How to Be Healthy

How can you be healthy? Start by learning the health standards. A **health standard** is a way to work toward good health. Here are the seven health standards.

1 Learn Health Facts

2 Get What You Need for Good Health

3 Make Health Plans

4 Think About Why You Do What You Do

5 Use Say NO Skills • Resolve Conflicts

6 Make Responsible Decisions™

7 Help Others to Be Safe and Healthy

HEALTH STANDARD 1 | Learn Health Facts

1. **Study and learn health facts.** A **health fact** is a true statement about health. These are health facts you might learn: Milk is a healthful drink. It makes bones strong. Soda is not a healthful drink. It has sugar in it.

2. **Ask questions if you do not understand health facts.** You might ask if milk has sugar in it. You might ask if soda makes bones strong. Your teacher or parent will answer your questions. Then you will be clear about health facts.

3. **Answer questions to show you understand health facts.** You might be asked what makes bones strong. You might say milk. You might be asked what has sugar in it. You might say soda. Your right answers show you understand health facts.

4. **Use health facts to practice life skills.**
A **life skill** is a healthful action you learn and practice for life. Here is a life skill: *I will eat healthful meals and snacks.* Suppose you want to practice this life skill. Remember these health facts: Milk is a healthful drink. Milk makes bones strong. Suppose you drink milk for a meal. You practice the life skill.

HEALTH STANDARD 2 | Get What You Need for Good Health

1. Name what you need for good health.
You need to know health facts. Suppose you want to care for your teeth. You need health facts about teeth. A **health product** is something you use for good health. A toothbrush is a health product. You need a toothbrush to brush teeth. A **health service** is help given by a person or place. A dentist is a health helper. To care for teeth, you might go to the dentist.

2. Find what you need for good health.
Find health facts in magazines and library books. Get health facts from a health helper. Find health products at a store. Get them from a parent or guardian. Know where to find health services. Find them in the phone book with a parent. Find help right away when you need it. Use the phone to call for help.

How to Call for Help

1. Find an adult.

2. Go to a phone if you cannot find an adult. Dial 9-1-1 or 0 (operator).

3. Give your name and address.

4. Tell what happened.

5. Listen to what the person tells you to do.

6. Do not hang up until you are told to do so.

3. **Check out what you need for good health.** Check out what you learn about health. Suppose someone on TV tells you an exercise will make your heart strong. Find out who this person is. Is she a doctor?

   Check out health products before you buy or use them. Suppose you need a toothbrush. Do you need a soft bristle or hard bristle?

   Check out health services. Suppose you need to have a checkup. Your parent or guardian can check out the doctor.

4. **Take action when something is not right.** Suppose you plan to buy a toothbrush. The package is open. Do not buy that toothbrush.

HEALTH STANDARD 3 | Make Health Plans

1. **Write the life skill you want to practice.** A **health plan** is a written plan that helps you practice a life skill. Look at **My Health Plan** on the next page. The **Life Skill** for this plan is: *I will take care of my teeth.*

2. **Give a plan for what you will do.** **My Plan** tells what you will do to practice the life skill. This plan says you will brush your teeth at least twice a day. It shows the correct way to brush your teeth.

3. **Keep track of what you do. What I Did** is a way to keep track of how well you follow the plan. The plan tells you to make checks in the teeth each time you brush your teeth.

4. **Tell how your plan worked.** How well did the person who made this plan do? Check out your health plan when you finish one. Did you stick to your plan?

My Health Plan

Life Skill I will take care of my teeth.

Name_____

Date_____

My Plan: I will brush my teeth at least twice a day.

What I Did: I will put a check in a tooth each time I brush that day.

There should be two checks in each tooth at the end of one week.

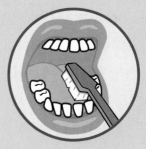

Sunday	Monday	Tuesday	Wednesday	Thursday	Friday	Saturday
	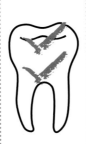	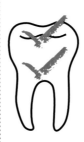	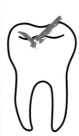		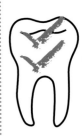	

HEALTH STANDARD 4
Think About Why You Do What You Do

1. **Name people and things that teach you to do things.** Your family and friends teach you to do things. You learn to do things by watching people on TV. You learn to do things by reading books and magazines. You learn to do things by listening to the radio. You learn to do things by seeing ads.

2. **Tell which ones help health. Tell which ones harm health.** Think about what your family and friends say and do. Think about what you listen to on the radio or when playing CDs. Think about what you hear and see in ads. Suppose you copy what other people say and do. Will your actions help health? Will they harm health?

3. Choose what helps your health.

Watch TV programs that show people with healthful actions. Read books and listen to CDs that tell ways to be healthy. Listen and copy the actions of people who want you to be healthy. Only choose things you see in ads that help health.

4. Avoid what harms your health.

Turn the TV channel if you see actions that harm health. Do not listen to CDs that have wrong words in them. Do not copy people whose actions harm health. Do not choose things in ads that harm health.

Buckle Up!
Seat belts Save Lives!

HEALTH STANDARD 5
- **Use Say NO Skills**
- **Resolve Conflicts**

Use Say NO Skills

A decision is a choice. A **wrong decision** is a choice you will not be proud of. **Say NO skills** are ways to say NO to wrong decisions.

1. **Look directly at the person.** Suppose a friend asked you to take a sip of beer. Look right at your friend.

2. **Say NO.** Say NO with a clear voice.

3. **Tell why you are saying NO.** You might say, "I want to be healthy," or "I want to obey my parents or guardian."

4. **Repeat your NO if you need to.** Suppose your friend keeps trying to get you to drink the beer. Say NO again. Give one or more of the same reasons.

5. **Do not change your mind.** Remember, it is never OK to make a wrong decision. Be firm. You will be proud of yourself. Your parents or guardian will be proud of you.

Resolve Conflicts

To resolve is to work out. A **conflict** is a disagreement. To **resolve conflict** is to work out a disagreement. Know how to resolve conflicts.

1. **Stay calm.** Take time to cool off. Count to ten. Take a deep breath.

2. **Listen to the other person's side of what happened.** Listen to what the person tells you. Try to understand how this person feels.

3. **Tell your side of what happened.** Tell your side without using mean words. Tell how you feel about what happened.

4. **Name different ways to work out the conflict.** Ask the other person to name ways. There might be different ways to work things out.

5. **Make a responsible choice.** Try to agree on a responsible choice. Your choice must be healthful and safe.

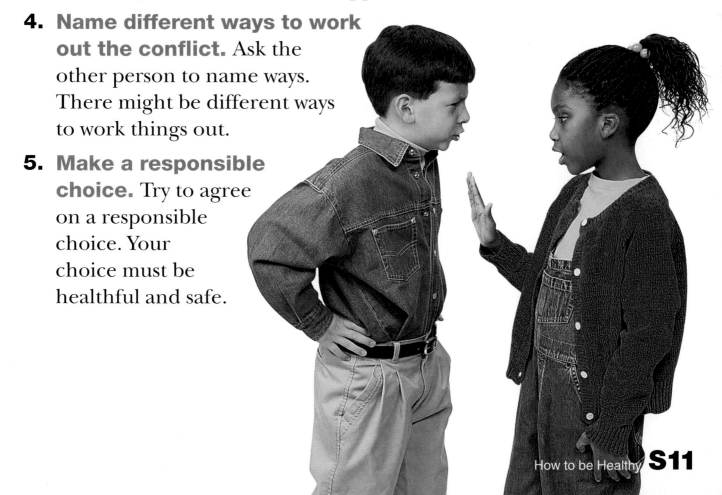

HEALTH STANDARD 6 | Make Responsible Decisions™

A **responsible decision** is a choice you will be proud of. Other people will respect you and think you have good character. **Respect** is thinking highly of someone. **Good character** is telling the truth, showing respect, and being fair. Know how to make responsible decisions.

1. **Tell what the choices are.** Suppose you are at a friend's house. Your friend wants to ride bikes. You do not have your bike. Your friend suggests that you ride double. Your choices are: 1. Agree to ride double. 2. Suggest doing something else.

2. **Use Guidelines for Making Responsible Decisions.™** Ask six questions about each choice before you make a decision. YES answers tell you a decision is responsible. NO answers tell you a decision is not responsible.

Guidelines for Making Responsible Decisions™

- **Is it healthful to ride double?** — **NO.** I might fall off the bike and get hurt.

- **Is it safe to ride double?** — **NO.** I might have an accident.

- **Do I follow rules and laws if I ride double?** — **NO.** It is against the law to ride double.

- **Do I show respect for myself and others if I ride double?** — **NO.** I put myself and my friend in danger.

- **Do I follow my family's guidelines if I ride double?** — **NO.** My family expects me to follow safety rules.

- **Do I show good character if I ride double?** — **NO.** Good character is about making responsible decisions.

3. **Tell what the responsible decision is.** You have answered NO to one or more of the six questions. Riding double is not a responsible decision. The responsible decision is to suggest doing something else.

4. **Tell what happens if you make this decision.** If you do something else, you will be proud of yourself. Your friend will respect you for making a responsible decision.

HEALTH STANDARD 7
Help Others to Be Safe and Healthy

Think about your family and friends. Think about other children in your school. Think about people who live near you. You can help others be safe and healthy.

1. **Choose a safe, healthful action.** There are many actions you might choose. You can choose to stay away from cigarette smoke.

2. **Tell others about the safe, healthful action.** Find health facts and share them with others. For example, you might tell others it is healthful to stay away from cigarette smoke. Breathing this smoke makes your heart beat faster.

3. **Do the safe, healthful action.** Stay away from cigarette smoke. Sit in places where no smoking is allowed. Others will see what you do. They might copy your healthful and safe actions.

4. Help others do the safe, healthful action. Think of ways to help others do the safe, healthful action. You might make a poster. The poster might say, "Stay away from cigarette smoke." It tells others to do the safe, healthful action.

Say YES to Good Health!

Good health is

- taking care of your body,
- taking care of your mind,
- sharing feelings,
- and getting along with others.

Good health helps you have success in school. Success in school means doing the very best you can do in school. Practice the health standards. Then you can have good health and success in school.

Macmillan/McGraw-Hill

Totally Awesome® Health

Linda Meeks
The Ohio State University

Philip Heit
The Ohio State University

Macmillan McGraw-Hill

New York   Farmington

Credits

Cover Design and Illustration: Devost Design

Cover Photo: PhotoDisc

Photos: *All photographs are by Macmillan/McGraw-Hill (MMH); Roman Sapecki; Lew Lause; and Ken Karp for MMH, except as noted below.*
Front Matter: S1: Tom & Dee Ann McCarthy/Corbis/The Stock Market; S2 - S3: PhotoDisc; S4: B. Daemmrich/Stock Boston; S5: Tony Freeman/Photo Edit; S8: bc. David Young-Wolff/PhotoEdit; bli. Michael Krasowitz/FPG; bli. bkgd. Ken Briggs/Stone; bl. David Toase/PhotoDisc; S9: bl. Frank Whitney/The Image Bank; bli. James Darell/Stone; S14: PhotoDisc; S16: bc. Tony Freeman/Photo Edit; br. PhotoDisc; bl: B. Daemmrich/The Image Works. Unit 4: 93: trc. PhotoDisc.

Illustrations: Jennifer King, Dave Odell, S.I. International Studio

Unit 10 outlines emergency care procedures that reflect the standard of knowledge and accepted practices in the United States at the time this book was published. It is the teacher's responsibility to stay informed of changes in emergency care procedures in order to teach current accepted practices. The teacher also can recommend that students gain complete, comprehensive training from courses offered by the American Red Cross.

Macmillan/McGraw-Hill

A Division of The McGraw·Hill Companies

Published by Macmillan/McGraw-Hill, of McGraw-Hill Education, a division of The McGraw-Hill Companies, Inc., Two Penn Plaza, New York, New York 10121.

Printed in the United States of America

ISBN 0-02-280433-1 / 2

    4 5 6 7 8 9 055 07 06 05 04

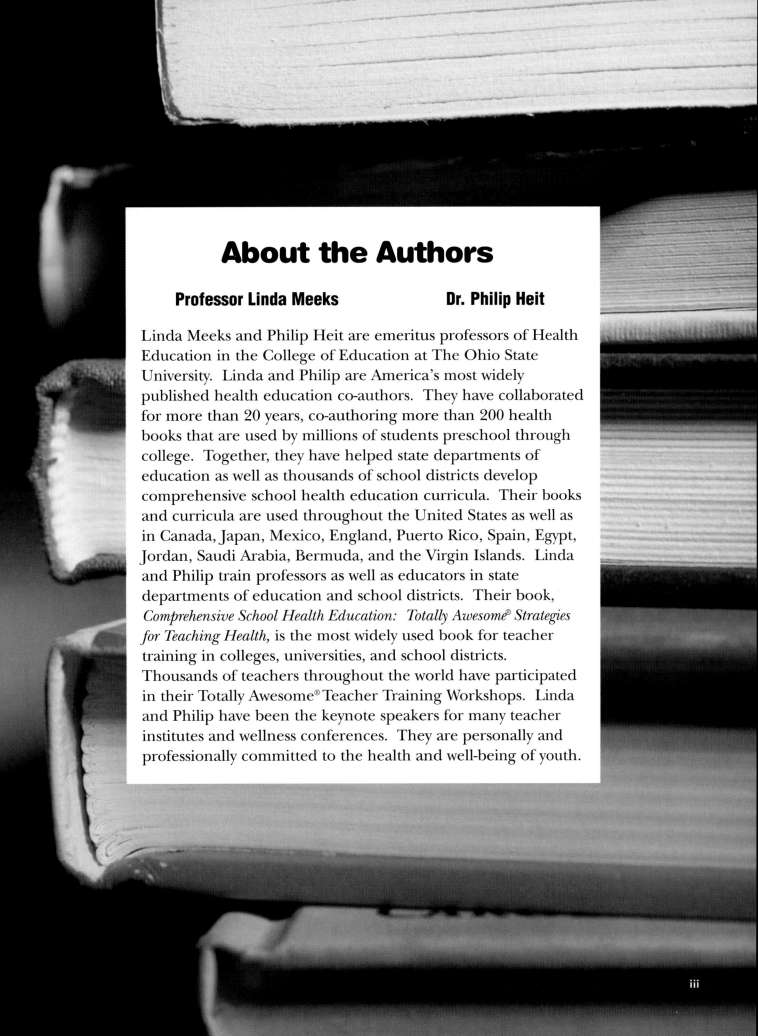

About the Authors

Professor Linda Meeks   Dr. Philip Heit

Linda Meeks and Philip Heit are emeritus professors of Health
Education in the College of Education at The Ohio State
University. Linda and Philip are America's most widely
published health education co-authors. They have collaborated
for more than 20 years, co-authoring more than 200 health
books that are used by millions of students preschool through
college. Together, they have helped state departments of
education as well as thousands of school districts develop
comprehensive school health education curricula. Their books
and curricula are used throughout the United States as well as
in Canada, Japan, Mexico, England, Puerto Rico, Spain, Egypt,
Jordan, Saudi Arabia, Bermuda, and the Virgin Islands. Linda
and Philip train professors as well as educators in state
departments of education and school districts. Their book,
*Comprehensive School Health Education: Totally Awesome® Strategies
for Teaching Health,* is the most widely used book for teacher
training in colleges, universities, and school districts.
Thousands of teachers throughout the world have participated
in their Totally Awesome® Teacher Training Workshops. Linda
and Philip have been the keynote speakers for many teacher
institutes and wellness conferences. They are personally and
professionally committed to the health and well-being of youth.

Medical Reviewers

Donna Bacchi, M.D., M.P.H.
Director, Division of
  Community Pediatrics
Texas Tech University
  Health Sciences Center
Lubbock, Texas

Albert J. Hart, Jr., M.D.
Mid-Ohio OB-GYN, Inc.
Westerville, Ohio

Reviewers

Kymm Ballard, M.A.
Physical Education, Athletics,
  and Sports Medicine
  Consultant
North Carolina Department
  of Public Instruction
Raleigh, North Carolina

Kay Bridges
Health Educator
Gaston County Public
  Schools
Gastonia, North Carolina

Lillie Burns
HIV/AIDS Prevention
  Education
Education Program
  Coordinator
Louisiana Department of
  Education
Baton Rouge, Louisiana

Deborah Carter-Hinton
Physical Education Health
  Resource Specialist
Joliet Public Schools
Joliet, Illinois

Anthony S. Catalano, Ph.D.
K-12 Health Coordinator
Melrose Public Schools
Melrose, Massachusetts

Galen Cole, M.P.H., Ph.D.
Division of Health
  Communication
Office of the Director
Centers for Disease Control
  and Prevention
Atlanta, Georgia

Brian Colwell, Ph.D.
Professor
Department of HLKN
Texas A&M University
College Station, Texas

Tommy Fleming, Ph.D.
Director of Health and
  Physical Education
Texas Education Agency
Austin, Texas

Elizabeth Gallun, M.A.
Specialist, Health and
  Physical Education
Office of Instructional
  Development
Maryland Department of
  Education
Baltimore, Maryland

Mary Gooding
Health Instructor
Tom Joy Elementary School
Nashville, Tennessee

Linda Harrill-Rudisill, M.A.
Chairperson of Health
  Education
Southwest Middle Schools
Gastonia, North Carolina

Janet Henke
Middle School Team Leader
Baltimore County Public
  Schools
Baltimore, Maryland

Russell Henke
Coordinator of Health
Montgomery County Public
  Schools
Rockville, Maryland

Robin Kimball
Belle Isle Enterprise
  Middle School
Oklahoma City, Oklahoma

Joe Leake, CHES
Curriculum Specialist
Baltimore City Public
  Schools
Baltimore, Maryland

Mary Marks, Ph.D.
Coordinator, Health and
  Physical Education
Fairfax County Public
  Schools
Falls Church, Virginia

Darlene Y. Nall
Health and Physical
  Education Instructor
Metro Nashville/Davidson
  County Public Schools
Nashville, Tennessee

Debra Ogden, M.A.
Coordinator of Health,
  Physical Education, Driver
  Education, and Safe and
  Drug-Free Programs
Collier County Public
  Schools
Naples, Florida

Merita Thompson, Ed.D.
Professor of Health
  Education
Eastern Kentucky University
Richmond, Kentucky

Linda Wright, M.A.
Project Director
HIV/AIDS Education
  Program
District of Columbia
  Public Schools
Washington, D.C.

Unit 1

Mental and Emotional Health

Lesson 1 Good Health **4**

What Are Reasons I Need Good Health? 5

   Activity: What Are Ways to Have a Healthy Mind? . . 6

What Are Reasons to Practice Life Skills? 7

How Do I Make a Health Plan? 8

   My Health Plan 9

Lesson 1 Review 9

Lesson 2 Picture Yourself As a Winner 10

How Can I Be a Winner?........................11

How Can I Make Responsible Decisions? 12–13

How Can I Say NO to Wrong Decisions?........14

Activity: NO! NO! NO!........................15

Lesson 2 Review........................**15**

Lesson 3 Shine with Good Character 16

Activity: What Actions Show
I Have Good Character?........................17

What Should I Do If I Make a Mistake?........18

Guidelines for Making Responsible Decisions™ .. 19

Lesson 3 Review........................**19**

Lesson 4 Actions and Feelings 20

How Can I Share Feelings?........................21

What Can I Do If I Feel Angry? 22

What Can I Do If I Feel Afraid?........23

How Can I Have a Good Self-Concept? 24

Activity: Make a Feelings Mask........................25

Lesson 4 Review........................**25**

Lesson 5 Stress and Hard Times 26

What Can Stress Do to My Body?........27

How Can I Manage Stress?........28

My Health Plan: Manage My Stress........29

Activity: Bounce Back from Hard Times........30

Lesson 5 Review........................**31**

Unit 1 Review **32–33**

Unit 2

Family and Social Health

Lesson 6 How to Keep Peace 36

What Are Ways to Show Respect? 37

What Can I Do If I Have a Conflict? 38

Activity: Make a Peace Chain 39

How Can I Keep from Fighting? 40

Activity: Pledge Not to Fight 41

Lesson 6 Review 41

Lesson 7 All Aboard the Friend-Ship 42

How Can I Be a True Friend? 43

How Can I Choose Friends? 44

Activity: Even Friendships **45**

How Can I Make Responsible Decisions with Friends? 46

Activity: Count on Responsible Decisions with Friends **47**

Lesson 7 Review **47**

Lesson 8 Someone to Lean On 48

How Can I Get Along with My Family? 49

My Health Plan: Help with Family Chores **50**

How Can I Be Responsible for a Family Pet? 51

Lesson 8 Review **51**

Lesson 9 Family Changes 52

What Things Can I Talk About If I Have Family Changes? 53

How Can I Help with a Newborn Baby? 54

Activity: How to Hold a Newborn Baby **55**

Lesson 9 Review **55**

Unit 2 Review **56–57**

Unit 3

Growth and Development

Lesson 10 **All About Your Body** **60**

How Can I Take Care of My Lungs? 61

How Can I Take Care of My Heart and Blood Vessels? 62

   Activity: What Do Blood Cells Do? **63**

How Can I Take Care of My Stomach? 64–65

How Can I Take Care of My Brain and Nerves? 66

   **Activity: Why Do I Need to Wear
   a Safety Helmet?** **67**

Lesson 10 Review **67**

Lesson 11 You Are Growing 68

How Can I Help My Bones Grow and Become Strong? 69

How Can I Help My Muscles Grow and Become Strong? . 70–71

Activity: What Happens to
My Muscles When I Exercise? 71

What Habits Help Me Grow Up Healthy?.............. 72–73

Lesson 11 Review 73

Lesson 12 Older and Wiser 74

What Are the Special Needs of Older People? 75

What Are Ways I Can Help Older People
Who Have Special Needs? 76

Activity: Draw the Sign for
a Handicapped Space......................... 77

Lesson 12 Review 77

Lesson 13 Different and Alike 78

What Are Ways I Use My Left Brain and My Right Brain? 79

My Health Plan: Use Your Brain 80

How Can I Get Help with Learning? 81

Lesson 13 Review 81

Unit 3 Review 82–83

Lesson 14 **Use the Food Guide Pyramid** **86**

My Health Plan: Eat Breakfast 87

How Can I Use the Food Guide Pyramid? 88–89

How Can I Use the Dietary Guidelines? 90–91

Lesson 14 Review **91**

Lesson 15 Snack Attack **92**

How Can I Choose Healthful Snacks?. 93

How Can I Choose Healthful Fast Foods?. 94

Activity: Caffeine Hunt 95

Lesson 15 Review **95**

Lesson 16 Watch That Fat **96**

How Can I Keep from Being Overfat? 97

Activity: What's on a Food Label? 98

Activity: TV Ad Jingles. 99

Lesson 16 Review **99**

Lesson 17 Germs in Food **100**

How Can I Keep Germs Out of Food?. 101

How Can I Have Good Table Manners?. 102

Guidelines for Making
Responsible Decisions™ 103

Lesson 17 Review **103**

Unit 4 Review **104–105**

Unit 5

Personal Health and Physical Activity

Lesson 18 Check Me Out **108**

What Happens During an Eye Checkup? 109

What Happens During an Ear Checkup? 110

Activity: Make a Health Record **111**

Lesson 18 Review **111**

Lesson 19 Don't Forget to Brush and Floss **112**

How Can I Take Care of My Teeth? 113

My Health Plan: Floss Each Day **114**

Activity: My Teeth Book **115**

Lesson 19 Review **115**

Lesson 20 Look Sharp **116**

How Can I Look Sharp? 117

Why Do I Need Sleep and Rest? 118

Activity: Stars in Our Classroom **119**

Lesson 20 Review **119**

Lesson 21 Exercise and Get Fit **120**

Why Do I Need to Get Plenty of Exercise? 121

What Is the Correct Way to Stretch Muscles? 122

What Exercises Make My Muscles Strong? 123

What Is the Correct Way to Build Heart Fitness? 124–125

Activity: Practice for the President's Challenge **126–127**

Lesson 21 Review **127**

Lesson 22 Exercise in Safe Ways **128**

How Can I Exercise in Safe Ways? 129

How Can I Be a Good Sport? 130

Guidelines for Making Responsible Decisions™ **131**

Lesson 22 Review **131**

Unit 5 Review **132–133**

Unit **6**

Say NO!

Alcohol, Tobacco, and Other Drugs

Say NO!

Lesson 23 Medicine Safety **136**

When Do I Need Medicine?. 137

What Are Rules for Using Medicine in Safe Ways? 138

Activity: The Medicine Cabinet 139

Lesson 23 Review **139**

Lesson 24 Alcohol...No Way! **140**

How Can Alcohol Harm My Health? 141

What People Can I Talk to If Someone
I Know Is a Problem Drinker? 142

**Guidelines for Making
Responsible Decisions™** **143**

Lesson 24 Review **143**

Lesson 25 Tobacco...No Way! **144**

How Can Tobacco Harm My Health? 145

How Can I Stay Away from Secondhand Smoke? 146

**Guidelines for Making
Responsible Decisions™** **147**

Lesson 25 Review **147**

Lesson 26 Drug-Free Pledge **148**

Why Should I Be Drug-Free? 149

Activity: Say NO to Drugs **150**

What Are Drugs That Are Against the Law? 151

Lesson 26 Review **151**

Unit 6 Review **152–153**

Unit 7

Communicable and Chronic Diseases

Lesson 27 Keep Germs Away **156**

How Can I Protect Myself and Others from Germs? 157

How Can I Get Well If I Have a Disease Caused by Germs? . 158

**Guidelines for Making
Responsible Decisions™** 159

Lesson 27 Review **159**

Lesson 28 Habits and Disease **160**

How Can I Prevent Heart Disease? 161

How Can I Prevent Cancer? 162

   Activity: I Love My Heart **163**

Lesson 28 Review **163**

Lesson 29 It's Hard to Breathe **164**

What Things Can Make Asthma and Allergies Worse? 165

How Can I Care for Allergies and Asthma? 166

   Activity: Allergy Guessing Game **167**

Lesson 29 Review **167**

Unit 7 Review **168–169**

Unit 8

Consumer and Community Health

Lesson 30 Don't Fall for Wrong Information **172**

Where Can I Find Health Facts? 173

What Questions Should I Ask When I See or Hear an Ad? 174

Activity: Check Out TV Ads 175

Lesson 30 Review **175**

Lesson 31 That's Entertainment 176

What Are Guidelines for Choosing Computer Games? 177

My Health Plan: Choose TV Shows
That Follow Guidelines for Healthful
Entertainment 178

Activity: Turn Off the TV 179

Lesson 31 Review **179**

Lesson 32 Know Health Helpers 180

What Do Health Helpers Do? 181

Activity: Steps to Become a Health Helper 182

What Does a Volunteer Do? 183

Lesson 32 Review **183**

Unit 8 Review **184–185**

Unit

9

Environmental Health

Lesson 33 Protect the Environment 188

How Can I Protect My Environment? 189

How Can I Keep My Environment Friendly? 190

Activity: Friendly Sash 191

Lesson 33 Review 191

Lesson 34 Don't Pollute **192**

How Can I Help Stop Pollution? 193

How Can I Save Energy and Resources? 194

Activity: Count on Recycling **195**

Lesson 34 Review **195**

Lesson 35 Turn Down the Noise **196**

Why Do I Need to Keep Noise Down? 197

My Health Plan: Keep Noise Down **198**

When Do I Need to Wear Ear Protectors? 199

Lesson 35 Review **199**

Unit 9 Review **200–201**

Unit 10

Injury Prevention and Safety

Lesson 36 Safety First **204**

How Can I Stay Safe at Home? 205

   Activity: Fire Safety Rules **206**

How Can I Stay Safe When I Travel? 207

How Can I Stay Safe When I Play? 208

   Activity: Stick with Playground Safety **209**

Lesson 36 Review **209**

Lesson 37 **Bully Beware** **210**
How Can I Stay Safe from a Bully? 211
How Can I Stay Safe from a Stranger? 212
What Are Rules If You Get an Unsafe Touch? 213
Lesson 37 Review **213**

Lesson 38 **Safe from Guns and Gangs** **214**
How Can I Stay Safe If I Find a Gun? 215
How Can I Stay Away from Gangs? 216
Guidelines for Making Responsible Decisions™ 217
Lesson 38 Review **217**

Lesson 39 **A Guide to First Aid** **218**
My Health Plan: Call for Help 219
What Should I Do If I Get a Cut? 220
What Should I Do If I Have a Nosebleed? 221
What Should I Do If an Animal Bites Me? 222
What Should I Do If I Get a Bee Sting? 223
Lesson 39 Review **223**

Unit 10 Review **224–225**

Unit 1

Mental and Emotional Health

Lesson 1
Good Health

Lesson 2
Picture Yourself As a Winner

Lesson 3
Shine with Good Character

Lesson 4
Actions and Feelings

Lesson 5
Stress and Hard Times

PRACTICE

HEALTH STANDARD 1

Learn Health Facts

Practice this standard at the end of this unit.

1. **Study and learn health facts.** Tell two body changes when you feel stress.

2. **Ask questions if you do not understand health facts.**
   Ask your teacher a question about stress.

3. **Answer questions to show you understand health facts.** Answer this question: Why does too much stress make you tired?

4. **Use health facts to practice life skills.** Tell how you will practice this life skill: *I will manage stress.*

Good Health

Life Skills

- **I will take care of my health.**
- **I will choose actions for a healthy mind.**
- **I will practice life skills for health.**

This book was written for you. Reading this book will help you learn about your health. You will learn what you can do to have good health.

What You Will Be Able to Do

- Tell reasons you need good health.
- Tell ways to have a healthy mind.
- Tell reasons to practice life skills.
- Tell steps to make a health plan.

Words You Will Learn

- **Good health** is taking care of your body, taking care of your mind, sharing feelings, and getting along with others.

- A **life skill** is a healthful action you learn and practice for life.

- A **health plan** is a written plan that helps you practice a life skill.

What Are Reasons I Need Good Health?

Good health is

• taking care of your body,

• taking care of your mind,

• sharing feelings,

• and getting along with others.

You take care of your body when you exercise and eat healthful foods. You take care of your mind when you read and work puzzles. You share feelings when you hug a family member. You get along with others when you share and take turns.

4 Reasons You Need Good Health

1. To play without getting tired

2. To do well in school

3. To enjoy playing with friends

4. To enjoy being with family members

What Are Ways to Have a Healthy Mind?

Activity

What You Will Need: Different colors of paper, crayons, and tape

1. **Read the Top Ten List of Ways to Have a Healthy Mind below.**

2. **Write one way to have a healthy mind on your sheet of colored paper.** Your teacher will tell you which one to write. Decorate your sheet of paper.

3. **Tape your sheet of paper to the papers of nine other classmates.** Hang this Top Ten List of Ways to Have a Healthy Mind in the classroom.

Top Ten List of Ways to Have a Healthy Mind

1. Put together a puzzle.

2. Read a book.

3. Work a math problem.

4. Go to the library.

5. Find out the meaning of a word you do not know.

6. Play a board game.

7. Learn all the words to a new song.

8. Write a letter.

9. Learn a new fact about health.

10. Watch a TV show about science.

What Are Reasons to Practice Life Skills?

You have learned reasons why you need good health. Knowing why you need good health is not enough. You must take action. A **life skill** is a healthful action you learn and practice for life.

This is a life skill: **I will get plenty of exercise.**

2 Reasons to Practice Life Skills

1. To have healthful habits
2. To stay in good health now and when you are older

I PRACTICE **LIFE SKILLS** TO STAY IN GOOD HEALTH.

How Do I Make a Health Plan?

A **health plan** is a written plan that helps you practice a life skill. Look at the health plan on the next page.

Suppose you want to make a health plan. There are three steps.

1. Write the life skill you want to practice.

2. Give a plan for what you will do.

3. Keep track of what you do.

4. Tell how your plan worked.

I will make a health plan to get plenty of exercise.

My Health Plan

Use the same life skill. Make your own Health Plan.

 **Life Skill**

I will get plenty of exercise.

Name_____

Date _____

My Plan: I will exercise five days a week. I will choose exercises that keep my heart healthy. I will do exercises that I enjoy.

- swimming
- skating
- tumbling
- biking
- playing baseball
- running

What I Did: I will write on my calendar the name of the exercise I did each day.

Monday _I rode my bike._____

Tuesday _____

Wednesday _____

Thursday _____

Friday _____

Lesson 1

Review

Health Questions

1. What are four reasons you need good health? **page 5**

2. What are three ways to have a healthy mind? **page 6**

3. What are two reasons to practice life skills? **page 7**

4. What are four steps to make a health plan? **page 8**

Picture Yourself As a Winner

Life Skills

- I will make responsible decisions.
- I will say NO to wrong decisions.

Suppose someone followed you with a camera. This person took pictures of things you did. Would you be proud of your actions?

What You Will Be Able to Do

- Tell how to be a winner.
- Tell six questions to ask before you make a decision.
- Show ways to say NO to wrong decisions.

Words You Will Learn

- A **responsible decision** is a choice you will be proud of.

- **Respect** is thinking highly of someone.

- **Good character** is telling the truth, showing respect, and being fair.

- A **wrong decision** is a choice you will not be proud of.

- **Say NO skills** are ways to say NO to wrong decisions.

How Can I Be a Winner?

Suppose you run a race and come in first. You win the race. Suppose you are in a spelling bee. You spell the most words correctly. You win the spelling bee. You are proud of yourself. You feel like a winner.

But you do not have to be first in everything to be a winner. You can be a winner if you make responsible decisions. A **responsible decision** is a choice you will be proud of.

You are a winner when you make responsible decisions.

How Can I Make Responsible Decisions?

Take time to think before you make a decision. Think about what will happen if you make the decision.

Use the Guidelines for Making Responsible Decisions.™ Use the *Guidelines for Making Responsible Decisions*™ on the next page. Answer the six questions. Suppose you answer YES to all six questions. Then you make a responsible decision.

Health Words

Respect is thinking highly of someone.

Good character (KEHR·ik·tuhr) is telling the truth, showing respect, and being fair.

Guidelines for Making Responsible Decisions™

Six questions to ask before you make a decision

1. Is it healthful to . . . . **?**

2. Is it safe to . . . . **?**

3. Do I follow rules
and laws if I . . . . **?**

4. Do I show respect for
myself and others if I . . . . **?**

5. Do I follow my family's
guidelines if I . . . . **?**

6. Do I show good
character if I . . . . **?**

How Can I Say NO to Wrong Decisions?

A **wrong decision** is a choice you will not be proud of. Suppose someone tries to get you to make a wrong decision. What can you do?

Use say NO skills. **Say NO skills** are ways to say NO to wrong decisions.

Say NO!

Say NO Skills

1. Look directly at the person.

2. Say NO.

3. Tell why you are saying NO.

4. Repeat your NO if you need to.

5. Do not change your mind.

NO! NO! NO!

Activity

1. Your teacher will read the wrong actions in column one.

2. You will say the words in column two.

Wrong Decisions	What You Should Say
Smoking a cigarette	NO. I want to be healthy.
Riding double on your bike	NO. I want to be safe.
Jaywalking	NO. I want to follow rules and laws.
Calling someone a name	NO. I want to show respect for myself and others.
Coming home late	NO. I want to follow my family's guidelines.
Cheating in a game	NO. I want to have good character.

Lesson 2 Review

Health Questions

1. How can you be a winner? **page 11**

2. What are six questions to ask before you make a decision? **page 13**

3. What are five say NO skills? **page 14**

Shine with Good Character

Life Skill

- **I will show good character.**

Respect is thinking highly of someone. Do you respect yourself? Do other people respect you? You need to have good character to earn respect.

What You Will Be Able to Do

- Give examples of actions that show good character.

- Explain what you should do if you make a mistake.

Words You Will Learn

- **Respect** is thinking highly of someone.

- **Good character** is telling the truth, showing respect, and being fair.

- A **mistake** is something that is done wrong.

- An **excuse** is a reason you use to try to get out of being responsible for what you did.

What Actions Show I Have Good Character?

What You Will Need: Paper and pencil

1. **Number a sheet of paper from one to three.** Leave enough space between numbers to draw apples.

2. **Memorize the definition of good character.**

Good character is:
- telling the truth,
- showing respect,
- and being fair.

3. **Read the list of Actions That Show Good Character below.**

4. **Think of a time when you acted in each way.** Then draw a shiny apple next to the correct number on your paper.

Actions That Show Good Character
1. I tell the truth when I do something wrong.
2. I do not say bad things about others.
3. I do not cheat when I play games.

Activity

What Should I Do If I Make a Mistake?

A **mistake** is something that is done wrong. Everyone makes mistakes.

Be responsible if you make a mistake. Say you made a mistake. Tell your parent or guardian. Do not make excuses. An **excuse** is a reason you use to try to get out of being responsible for what you did.

Do something about the mistake. Suppose you pushed someone. Say you are sorry.

Do not make the same mistake again. Think of ways to keep from making the same mistake again.

Use...
Guidelines for Making Responsible Decisions™

Situation:

You are playing a card game with a friend. Your friend puts his cards down and goes to the kitchen to get a can of soda. It would help you win if you looked at your friend's cards.

Response:

Answer the questions in bold.

1. Is it healthful to look at your friend's cards?

2. Is it safe to look at your friend's cards?

3. **Do you follow rules and laws if you look at your friend's cards?**

4. **Do you show respect for your friend if you look at your friend's cards?**

5. Do you follow your family's guidelines if you look at your friend's cards?

6. **Do you show good character if you look at your friend's cards?**

What is the responsible decision?

Lesson 3

Review

Health Questions

1. What are three actions that show good character? **page 17**

2. What are three things you should do if you make a mistake? **page 18**

Actions and Feelings

Life Skill

• **I will share feelings.**

Feelings are the ways you feel inside. You have many different feelings. You might feel happy, sad, angry, or afraid. How do you share feelings?

What You Will Be Able to Do

• Tell ways to share feelings.

• Explain what to do if you are angry or afraid.

• Explain how to have a good self-concept.

Words You Will Learn

• **Feelings** are the ways you feel inside.

• **Angry** is feeling very upset with someone or something.

• **Afraid** is feeling scared.

• **Self-concept** is the feeling you have about yourself.

How Can I Share Feelings?

You can talk about your feelings.

Suppose you play baseball and hit the ball a long way. You feel happy. Suppose you are not asked to a friend's birthday party. You feel hurt. Talk to your parents or guardian about your feelings.

You can show your feelings with responsible actions.

Suppose you feel love for your aunt. You might hug her.

You can write or draw about your feelings.

Suppose your grandmother sent you a gift. You might write her a letter.

What Can I Do If I Feel Angry?

Angry is feeling very upset with someone or something. It's OK to feel angry.

Take time to cool off. This helps you think about what you will do or say.

Share your angry feelings in a healthful way. Choose responsible actions. Talk things out. Write about your angry feelings. Do not fight or say unkind things. Do not break anything.

Ask your parents or guardian to help you when you do not know how to share angry feelings. Do not keep your angry feelings to yourself.

What Can I Do If I Feel Afraid?

Afraid is feeling scared. Some children are afraid of the dark. Some children are afraid of spiders.

Tell your parents or guardian if you feel afraid. They will tell you how to stay safe if someone or something could harm you.

Protect yourself when someone or something could harm you. Stay away from strangers. Tell your parents or guardian about a stranger right away.

Tell yourself not to be afraid when you are not in danger. Suppose you are afraid to go to sleep in the dark. Keep saying to yourself, "Nothing will harm me. I am safe."

Tell your parents or guardian if you feel afraid.

How Can I Have a Good Self-Concept?

Self-concept is the feeling you have about yourself. There are two things you can do to have a good self-concept.

Share your feelings in healthful ways. Suppose you are angry. Do not punch or kick someone. Do not break anything. Talk things out. Then you can feel good about yourself.

Choose responsible actions. Suppose your parents or guardian tell you to call them if you go inside a friend's home. Be sure to call them. Then you can feel good about yourself.

Make a Feelings Mask

What You Will Need: Newspaper, flour, water, bucket, and paints

1. **Tear small pieces of paper into a small bucket.**

2. **Add papier-mâché paste to it.** Let it soak until it feels soft. Mix it.

3. **Shape it into a mask.**

4. **Paint the mask to show feelings.**

Papier-Mâché Paste

Mix one glass of flour with three glasses of water. Stir until the mixture is smooth and creamy. The paste is ready to use.

Activity

Lesson 4

Review

Health Questions

1. What are three ways to share feelings? **page 21**

2. What are three things you can do if you feel angry? **page 22**

3. What are three things you can do if you feel afraid? **page 23**

4. What are two things you can do to have a good self-concept? **page 24**

Stress and Hard Times

Life Skills

- **I will manage stress.**
- **I will bounce back from hard times.**

Have you ever worried about going to the dentist? Have you ever gotten on a scary ride at the fair? Have you ever had a disagreement with a friend? You might have felt stress.

What You Will Be Able to Do

- Tell what stress can do to your body.

- Make a health plan to show ways you can manage stress.

Words You Will Learn

- **Stress** is the way your body reacts to strong feelings.

- A **stress plan** is a health plan to show how you will manage stress.

What Can Stress Do to My Body?

Stress is the way your body reacts to strong feelings. Your body changes when you feel stress. Your heart beats faster than usual. You breathe faster than usual. Sugar stored in your body goes into your blood. This sugar gives you more energy.

Your mouth might get dry. Your hands might get sweaty. Your muscles might get tight.

Too much stress can make you tired. Then you might get sick. You might have an accident.

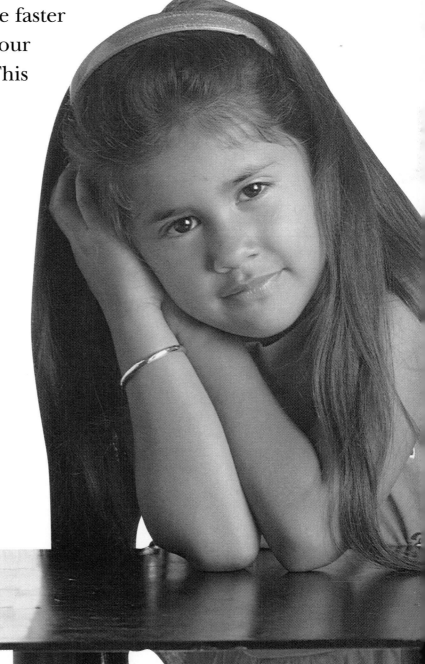

How Can I Manage Stress?

A **stress plan** is a health plan to show how you will manage stress.

Talk to your parents or guardian.

They can support you.

Get plenty of rest and sleep.

Then you will not be tired. You will not get sick or have accidents.

Spend time with your friends.

Talk with friends about things that bother you. Do fun things with friends.

Relax by getting exercise.

Exercise can help tight muscles. It uses up the extra sugar that gets in the blood. It sends blood to your brain. This helps you think clearly.

My Health Plan

Use the same life skill. Make your own Health Plan.

Manage My Stress

I will manage stress.

Name _____

Date _____

My Plan: These are ways I can manage stress.

- **I will talk to my parents or guardian.**
- **I will get plenty of rest and sleep.**
- **I will spend time with my friends.**
- **I will relax by getting exercise.**

What I Did:

Sunday	*I rode my bicycle to relax.*
Monday	
Tuesday	
Wednesday	
Thursday	
Friday	
Saturday	

Bounce Back from Hard Times

Activity

What You Will Need: A large rubber ball

1. **Think about a hard time when you felt stressed.** You can bounce back from hard times.

2. **Learn how to bounce back from hard times.** Bounce the rubber ball four times. This is what you say when you drop the ball and make it bounce.

Bounce 1:
Talk to my parents or guardian.

Bounce 3:
Spend time with my friends.

Bounce 4:
Exercise.

Bounce 2:
Get plenty of rest and sleep.

Pets and Stress

Do you have a pet? Having a pet can help you manage stress. You can hold your pet when you feel stress. Being close can make you feel better.

You can talk to your pet. Sometimes it helps to talk aloud about what bothers you. Pets help you feel loved.

Lesson 5
Review

Health Questions

1. What can stress do to your body?
   page 27

2. What are ways you can manage stress?
   page 28

Health Questions

1. What are four steps to make a health plan? **Lesson 1 page 8**

2. What are six questions to ask before you make a decision? **Lesson 2 page 13**

3. What are three things you should do if you make a mistake? **Lesson 3 page 18**

4. What are two things you can do to have a good self-concept? **Lesson 4 page 24**

5. What are ways you can manage stress? **Lesson 5 page 28**

Guidelines for Making Responsible Decisions™

You step on your brother's toy and break it. Your friend tells you to say someone else did it. **Answer the questions in bold.**

1. Is it healthful to blame someone else?

2. Is it safe to blame someone else?

3. Do you follow rules and laws if you blame someone else?

4. **Do you show respect for your brother if you blame someone else?**

5. **Do you follow your family's guidelines if you blame someone else?**

6. **Do you show good character if you blame someone else?**

What is the responsible decision?

Health Words

Number a sheet of paper from 1–5. Write the word that belongs in the blank. Use the health words in the box.

> life skill
>
> say NO skills
>
> excuse
>
> self-concept
>
> stress plan

1. _____ is the feeling you have about yourself. **Lesson 4**

2. An _____ is a reason you use to try to get out of being responsible for what you did. **Lesson 3**

3. A _____ _____ is a health plan to show how you will manage stress. **Lesson 5**

4. A _____ _____ is a healthful action you learn and practice for life. **Lesson 1**

5. _____ _____ _____ are ways to say NO to wrong decisions. **Lesson 2**

Health Skills

Express Yourself

Draw a picture of an angry face. Tell one thing that makes you feel angry.

Learn on Your Own

Check out a library book on health. Read it with your parent or guardian.

Use Thinking Skills

Why do you want to have good character?

Be a Good Citizen

Memorize the six questions to ask before you make a decision. Promise your parents or guardian that you will use them.

Family and Social Health

Lesson 6
How to Keep Peace
Lesson 7
All Aboard the Friend-Ship
Lesson 8
Someone to Lean On
Lesson 9
Family Changes

PRACTICE

HEALTH STANDARD 5 | **Resolve Conflicts**

Practice this standard at the end of this unit.

Pair up with a classmate. Pretend your classmate kicked your dog.

1. **Stay calm.** Tell how you can stay calm.

2. **Listen to the other person's side of what happened.** Ask your classmate to tell what happened.

3. **Tell your side of what happened.** Tell what you saw your classmate do. Tell how you feel.

4. **Name different ways to work out the conflict.** Tell a way. Have your classmate tell a way.

5. **Make a responsible choice.** Tell what the responsible choice is.

How to Keep Peace

Life Skills

- **I will show respect for others.**
- **I will work out conflict.**

You spend time with family members. You go to school and play with other children. How do you get along with others? What do you do when you disagree?

What You Will Be Able to Do

- Tell ways to show respect for others.
- Explain what to do if you have a conflict.
- Tell ways to keep from fighting.

Words You Will Learn

- **Respect** is thinking highly of someone.
- A **conflict** is a disagreement.
- A **fight** is a disagreement in which you pull hair, kick, push, punch, or pinch.

What Are Ways to Show Respect?

Respect is thinking highly of someone. You get along better when you show respect.

Speak in a kind way. Do not yell or say mean things. Do not call anyone bad names. Do not make jokes about anyone.

Show kind actions. Use good manners. Say, "Excuse me," if you bump into someone. Do not push or trip other children when you play. Share and take turns.

Follow rules and laws. Do not ask other children to break rules and laws. This keeps you and others safe.

What Can I Do If I Have a Conflict?

A **conflict** is a disagreement. Everyone has conflicts sometimes. It is OK to have a conflict. But you must work out a conflict.

What to Do If You Have a Conflict

1. Stay calm.

2. Listen to the other person's side of what happened.

3. Tell your side of what happened.

4. Name different ways to work out the conflict.

5. Make a responsible choice.

Make a Peace Chain

Activity

What You Will Need: Construction paper, crayons, tape or stapler

1. **Each child in your class will cut a strip of paper.**

2. **Each child will write on his or her strip of paper.** Write one of the five things you can do if you have a conflict.

3. **Staple the strips of paper together to make a Peace Chain.**

STAY CALM

What will happen if you tear out one of the links in the Peace Chain?

How Can I Keep from Fighting?

A **fight** is a disagreement in which you pull hair, kick, push, punch, or pinch. It is wrong to fight. You might hurt someone else. You might get hurt if you fight.

What to Do If Someone Wants You to Fight

1. Say you do not want to fight.

2. Say you were wrong if you did something wrong. Offer to make up for what you did.

3. Wait until you are calm and talk things out.

4. Get away if the person tries to harm you.

5. Ask a parent, guardian, or other adult for help.

Pledge Not to Fight

What You Will Need: Paper and pencil

1. Copy the pledge on a piece of paper.

2. Take the pledge home to your parents or guardian.

Pledge Not to Fight

I pledge that if I disagree,
I'll solve my conflict peacefully.
I will listen and stay calm.
I'll say I am sorry if I am wrong.
I will not push, punch, pinch, or kick.
To work things out will be my pick.
I will not say mean things for spite.
I will say NO. I will not fight.

Lesson 6
Review

Health Questions

1. What are three ways to show respect? **page 37**

2. What are five things you can do if you have a conflict? **page 38**

3. What are five things you can do if someone wants you to fight? **page 40**

All Aboard the Friend-Ship

- **I will help others take care of their health.**
- **I will make responsible decisions with friends.**

Suppose you saw a large ship. The captain of the ship asked you to come aboard. The captain told you to bring your friends. Do you have friends you could ask?

What You Will Be Able to Do

- Tell how to be a true friend.
- Tell ways to choose friends.
- Tell six questions to ask when you make decisions with friends.

Words You Will Learn

- A **true friend** is a friend who is responsible and who cares about you.

- A **responsible decision** is a choice you will be proud of.

- An **even friendship** is a friendship in which friends take turns sharing and choosing.

How Can I Be a True Friend?

A **true friend** is a friend who is responsible and who cares about you. You can be a true friend to others.

Make responsible decisions when you are with a friend. A **responsible decision** is a choice you will be proud of. Then you and your friend will not get in trouble.

Show your friend you care. Help your friend take care of his or her health. For example, eat healthful snacks together.

Take turns with your friend. An **even friendship** is a friendship in which friends take turns sharing and choosing. Do some of the talking and some of the listening.

How Can I Choose Friends?

Choose friends whom your parents or guardians like. Your parents or guardians see how other children act. They see how other children treat you.

Choose friends who show respect for you. A friend should not say mean things to you. A friend should not try to start fights.

Choose friends who want an even friendship. You and your friend should listen as well as talk. You and your friend should take turns choosing what to do.

Even Friendships

What You Will Need: Poster paper, paints or crayons

1. **Pair up with another child to make a poster.** Your poster will show four fun things to do together.

2. **Decide who will take the first turn.** This person will draw or paint something he or she likes to do.

3. **Have the other person take the next turn.** This person will draw or paint something he or she likes to do.

4. **Take turns again.**

5. **Talk about your poster.**
   Why is it good to take turns?
   Why is it best to have even friendships?

How Can I Make Responsible Decisions with Friends?

Use the *Guidelines for Making Responsible Decisions*™ with friends.

Suppose you answer NO to one or more questions. Do not make this decision. Do not let your friend change your mind.

Guidelines for Making Responsible Decisions™

Six questions to ask before you make a decision

1. Is it healthful to . . . . ?
2. Is it safe to . . . . ?
3. Do I follow rules and laws if I . . . . ?
4. Do I show respect for myself and others if I . . . . . . ?
5. Do I follow my family's guidelines if I . . . . ?
6. Do I show good character if I . . . . ?

Count on Responsible Decisions with Friends

What You Will Need: A string and six beads

1. **Make a string of beads with a partner.** Tie knots at both ends of the string.

2. **Have each partner hold one end of the string.** Push all six beads to one end.

3. **Your teacher will say a decision you can make together.** Ask the first question. Move the bead to the other side of the string if the answer is YES. Keep going. Stop if an answer is NO.

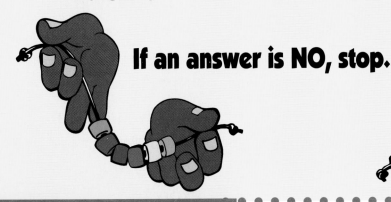

If an answer is NO, stop.

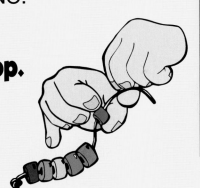

Lesson 7

Review

Health Questions

1. What are three ways to be a true friend? **page 43**

2. What are three ways to choose friends? **page 44**

3. What are six questions to ask when you make decisions with friends? **page 46**

Someone to Lean On

Life Skill

- **I will get along with my family.**

Do you hold the handrail when you climb stairs? The handrail gives you support. Family members can give you support, too. You can lean on them.

What You Will Be Able to Do

- Tell ways to get along with your family.
- Make a health plan to help with family chores.
- Tell ways to be responsible for a family pet.

Words You Will Learn

- Your **family** is the group of people to whom you are related.

- **Family guidelines** are rules your parents or guardians expect you to follow.

- A **chore** is a small job.

- A **pet** is an animal that is kept in the home.

How Can I Get Along with My Family?

Your **family** is the group of people to whom you are related. There are ways to get along with your family.

Follow family guidelines. **Family guidelines** are rules your parents or guardians expect you to follow. They might expect you to put your bike away. They might expect you to come home at a certain time.

Plan time to be with family members. Work and play with your family. Tell your family what happened at school each day. Ask family members what they did each day.

My Health Plan

Use the same life skill. Make your own Health Plan.

Help with Family Chores

 **Life Skill** I will get along with my family.

Name _____

Date _____

My Plan: I will help with family chores. A **chore** is a small job.

- I will keep my room clean.
- I will make my bed.
- I will set the table.
- I will help clean the dishes.

- I will take out the trash.
- I will dust the furniture.
- I will sweep the sidewalk, garage, or other place.

What I Did:

Sunday	I made my bed.
Monday	
Tuesday	
Wednesday	
Thursday	
Friday	
Saturday	

How Can I Be Responsible for a Family Pet?

A **pet** is an animal that is kept in the home. If you have a pet, be responsible for it.

Take care of your pet. Feed your pet. Keep your pet groomed. Brush its hair or coat. Keep your pet on your property. Keep it on a leash when it walks with you away from home.

Be kind to your pet. Never kick or hit a pet. Do not pull its tail or tease it. Remember to feed your pet.

- Never hit or kick a pet.
- Never pull a pet's ears or tail.
- Tell an adult if someone harms animals.

Lesson 8
Review

Health Questions

1. What are two ways to get along with your family? **page 49**

2. What are three chores you can do to help your family? **page 50**

3. What are two ways to be responsible for a family pet? **page 51**

Lesson 9

Family Changes

• I will share feelings about family changes.

Suppose you get used to something. You expect it always to be that way. But sometimes things change. Then you must do things in new ways.

What You Will Be Able to Do

• Tell things to talk about if you have family changes.

• Tell ways to help with a newborn baby.

Words You Will Learn

• A **divorce** is the end of a marriage.

• To **remarry** is to get married again.

• To **adopt** is to bring a child from other parents into your family.

What Things Can I Talk About If I Have Family Changes?

Some children have changes in their families. A child's family might move to a new city. A child's grandparent might die.

A child's parents might get a divorce. A **divorce** (duh·VOHRS) is the end of a marriage. The child might live with one parent. The child might see the other parent at certain times. A parent might remarry. To **remarry** is to get married again.

Things to Talk About If You Have Family Changes

1. What will happen next

2. Any fears you have

3. Ways your parents or guardian can help you

How Can I Help with a Newborn Baby?

Some children have newborn babies in their families. A mother or stepmother might give birth. A family might adopt a baby. To **adopt** is to bring a child from other parents into your family.

Share the attention of your parents or guardian. The baby needs a lot of care. You are loved even though you do not get all the attention.

Ask for ways you can help. You might get things for the person who is caring for the baby. You might put things away.

How to Hold a Newborn Baby

What You Will Need: A baby doll

1. **Feel the top of your head.** You feel the bones that make up the skull. A baby has a soft spot on the top of the head. The bones have not closed together yet. This leaves room for the baby's head to grow. Your teacher will show you where the soft spot is.

2. **Hold your baby doll and support its head.** This protects the soft spot. It protects the baby's brain from harm.

Lesson 9

Review

Health Questions

1. What are three things to talk about if you have family changes? **page 53**

2. What are two ways to help with a newborn baby? **page 54**

Unit 2

Review

Health Questions

1. What are five things you can do if someone wants you to fight? **Lesson 6 page 40**

2. What are three ways to choose friends? **Lesson 7 page 44**

3. What are six questions to ask when you make decisions with friends? **Lesson 7 page 46**

4. What are two ways to get along with your family? **Lesson 8 page 49**

5. What are three things to talk about if you have family changes? **Lesson 9 page 53**

Guidelines for Making Responsible Decisions™

A classmate pushes you. You are angry. Should you punch your classmate? **Answer the questions in bold.**

1. **Is it healthful to punch your classmate?**

2. **Is it safe to punch your classmate?**

3. **Do you follow rules and laws if you punch your classmate?**

4. **Do you show respect if you punch your classmate?**

5. **Do you follow your family's guidelines if you punch your classmate?**

6. **Do you show good character if you punch your classmate?**

What is the responsible decision?

Health Words

Number a sheet of paper from 1–5. Write the word that belongs in the blank. Use the health words in the box.

> conflict
>
> even friendship
>
> true friend
>
> family guidelines
>
> remarry

1. A _____ _____ is a friend who is responsible and who cares about you. **Lesson 7**

2. _____ _____ are rules your parents or guardians expect you to follow. **Lesson 8**

3. A _____ is a disagreement. **Lesson 6**

4. To _____ is to get married again. **Lesson 9**

5. An _____ _____ is a friendship in which friends take turns sharing and choosing. **Lesson 7**

Health Skills

Express Yourself

Make a thank-you card to give to a parent or guardian. Thank the person you chose for something he or she does for you.

Learn on Your Own

Find a book about friendship in the library. Read the book. Draw a picture to show what you learned.

Use Thinking Skills

Why is it best to have even friendships?

Be a Good Citizen

Ask your parents or guardian first. Do a chore for one of your neighbors.

Unit
3

Growth and Development

Lesson 10
All About Your Body

Lesson 11
You Are Growing

Lesson 12
Older and Wiser

Lesson 13
Different and Alike

PRACTICE
HEALTH STANDARD 7

Help Others to Be Safe and Healthy

Practice this standard at the end of this unit.

1. **Choose a safe, healthful action.** Drink plenty of water.

2. **Tell others your stand on the safe, healthful action.** Tell classmates you will drink 8 glasses of water a day. Tell them why.

3. **Do the safe, healthful action.** Keep a record of how many glasses of water you drink each day.

4. **Help others to do the safe, healthful action.** Make a poster. Draw 8 glasses of water. Write "Drink plenty of water every day."

All About Your Body

Life Skill

- **I will take care of my body.**

Your body has many parts. All of these parts belong to body systems. A body system is made up of the body parts that work together to do a certain job.

What You Will Be Able to Do

- Tell ways to take care of body parts.

Words You Will Learn

- **Lungs** are body parts that help move air in and out of your body.

- Your **heart** is a body part that pumps blood.

- Your **stomach** is a body part that helps change food so your body can use it.

- Your **brain** is the body part that sends and receives messages to and from all parts of your body.

- **Nerves** are body parts that carry messages to and from your brain to the rest of your body.

How Can I Take Care of My Lungs?

You breathe air through your mouth and nose. The air goes into your lungs. Your **lungs** are body parts that help move air in and out of your body. All body parts need air to stay alive.

Most people breathe in 10 to 20 times each minute. Your body needs more air when you move about. You breathe more often.

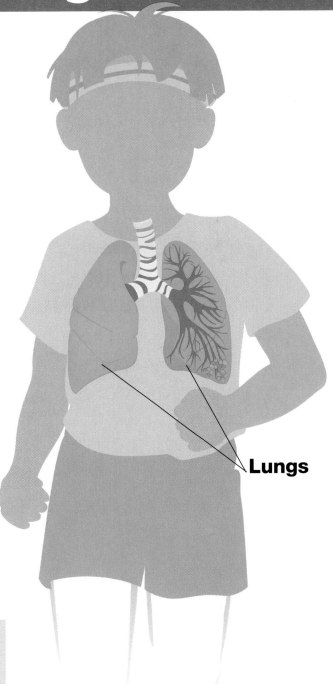

Lungs

Take Care of Your Lungs

• Stay away from smoke.

• Get plenty of exercise.

• Do not breathe glue or cleaners.

How Can I Take Care of My Heart and Blood Vessels?

Your **heart** is a body part that pumps blood. Your heart is at the center of your chest. It tips to the left a bit.

Blood travels through your body in blood vessels. Blood vessels are tubes that carry blood to and from your heart and body parts. This is how body parts get food and oxygen.

Heart

Blood vessels

Take Care of Your Heart and Blood Vessels

- Get plenty of exercise.
- Eat low-fat foods.
- Do not smoke.
- Stay away from smoke.

What Do Blood Cells Do?

What You Will Need: Red, blue, and white clay

1. **Make a red blood cell.** Blood is made up of tiny cells. Red blood cells carry oxygen to body parts. Flatten a ball of red clay on your desk. It will form a circle. Press your thumb in the middle of the circle. This is what a red blood cell looks like.

2. **Make a white blood cell.** White blood cells get rid of germs that get into the body. Flatten a ball of white clay on your desk. White cells have different shapes.

3. **Make your white blood cell gobble up a germ.** Make a very tiny ball of blue clay. This is a germ. Place it in the middle of the white cell. Close the white cell around it. White cells surround germs and gobble them up.

Red blood cells carry oxygen to body parts.

Activity

How Can I Take Care of My Stomach?

Your teeth chew and soften food. Food goes to your stomach when you swallow it. Your **stomach** is a body part that helps change food so your body can use it. Stomach juices work to change the food.

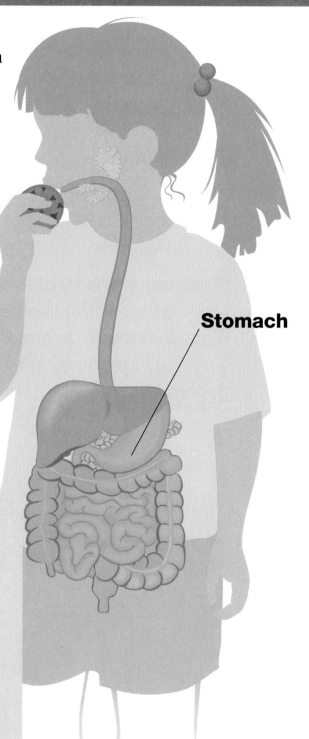

Stomach

Take Care of Your Stomach

• Drink plenty of water.

• Do not eat too many spicy foods.

• Chew food before you swallow it.

• Keep things other than food out of your mouth so you do not swallow them.

Why Do I Throw Up?

There are different reasons you throw up. Something might bother the lining of your stomach. You might see or smell something that bothers you. Being upset might cause you to throw up. Vomit, barf, puke, and upchuck are other words for throwing up.

Why Do I Burp?

You swallow air when you eat and drink. This adds gas to your stomach. Stomach juices add more gas. Gas must get out of your stomach. You burp to get rid of gas. Belch is another word for burp.

How Can I Take Care of My Brain and Nerves?

Your **brain** is the body part that sends and receives messages to and from all parts of your body.

Nerves are body parts that carry messages to and from your brain to the rest of your body. Nerves carry messages to help you see, hear, smell, taste, touch, and move.

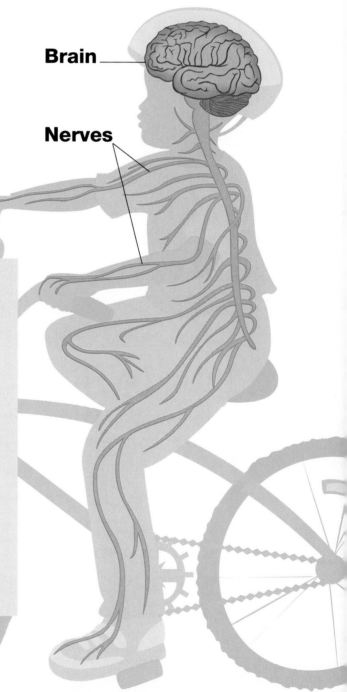

Brain

Nerves

Protect Your Brain and Nerves

- Wear a helmet if you ride a bike or skate.

- Wear a helmet in the batter's box if you play baseball.

- Do not swallow poison.

- Do not breathe fumes from glue or cleaners.

- Wear a safety belt when you ride in a car.

Why Do I Need to Wear a Safety Helmet?

What You Will Need: Two peanuts in their shells, cotton, and a piece of foil

1. **Feel the shell that protects the peanut.** Your skull is like a peanut shell. It protects your brain.

2. **Crack open the shell of the peanut.** The peanuts inside are like your brain.

3. **Learn how a safety helmet protects the skull and brain.** Put cotton around another peanut. Then wrap it with a piece of foil. This is like a safety helmet. A safety helmet has padding and a hard coating.

Activity

Lesson 10 Review

Health Questions

1. What are three ways to take care of your lungs? **page 61**

2. What are four ways to take care of your heart and blood vessels? **page 62**

3. What are four ways to take care of your stomach? **page 64**

4. What are five ways to protect your brain and nerves? **page 66**

You Are Growing

Life Skills

- I will learn ways my body changes.
- I will choose habits to grow up healthy.

You are growing. To **grow** is to become bigger. Your body parts will grow. You will gain weight and grow taller.

What You Will Be Able to Do

- Tell ways to help your bones grow and become strong.
- Tell ways to help your muscles grow and become strong.

Words You Will Learn

- To **grow** is to become bigger.
- **Bones** are strong, hard body parts that support the soft body parts.
- **Muscles** are body parts that help you move.
- A **habit** is the way you do something most of the time.

How Can I Help My Bones Grow and Become Strong?

Bones are strong, hard body parts that support the soft body parts. They form a frame inside your body.

You have many bones in your body. Some bones are long. Some bones are short. Your bones have different shapes.

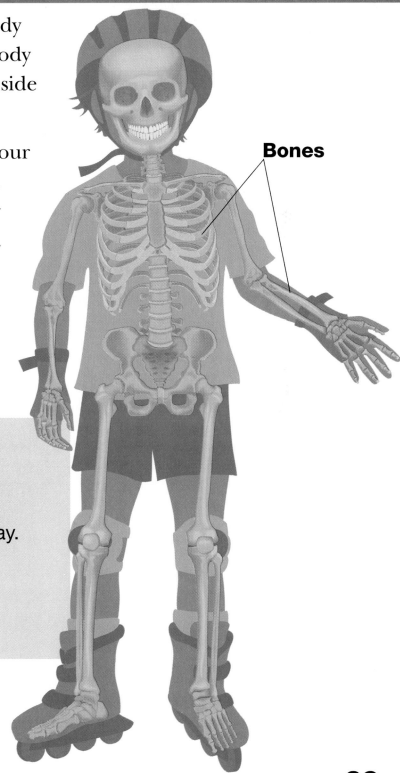

Bones

Help Your Bones Grow and Become Strong

• Wear safety equipment to protect bones when you play.

• Drink milk.

• Eat foods made with milk.

• Get plenty of exercise.

How Can I Help My Muscles Grow and Become Strong?

Muscles are body parts that help you move. Clench your fist. You will see the muscles in your hand, wrist, and arm move. Blink. You will feel the muscles in your eyelids move.

Suppose you run, jump, or swim. Muscles work with your bones to help you move. Your muscles power every move you make.

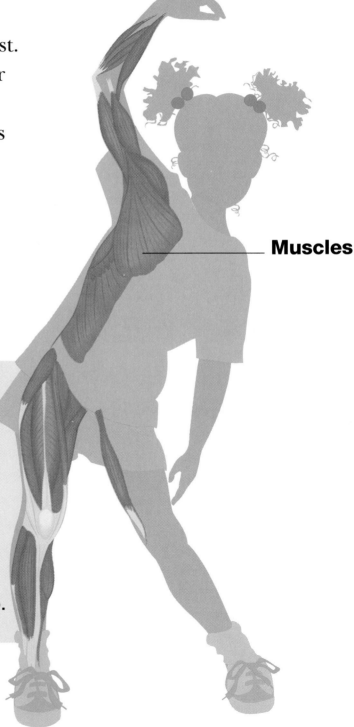

Muscles

Help Your Muscles Grow and Become Strong

- Stretch your muscles at least two to three times a week.

- Get plenty of exercise.

- Drink milk.

- Eat green leafy vegetables and foods from the milk group.

Why Do I Get a Muscle Cramp?

Suppose you do not use muscles for a while. A muscle might become hard and tight. You get a muscle cramp. Ouch! Gently rub and stretch the muscle.

What Happens to My Muscles When I Exercise?

Activity

What You Will Need: Five straws and plastic wrap

1. **Show what muscles look like.** Put plastic wrap around three straws. This is what muscles look like.

2. **Find out what happens to muscles when you exercise.** Take two more straws. Put them with the first three straws. Put plastic wrap around all five straws. Muscles get thick when you exercise. Then you are stronger.

What Habits Help Me Grow Up Healthy?

A **habit** is the way you do something most of the time. Do you exercise most days after school? If you do, exercise is a habit.

Some habits help you grow up healthy. If you do them now, you will be healthy when you grow up.

Ten Habits That Help You Grow Up Healthy

1. Eat breakfast every day.

2. Choose healthful foods.

3. Get plenty of exercise.

4. Do not smoke or breathe in smoke.

5. Get plenty of rest and sleep.

6. Get checkups.

7. Mix work with play.

8. Read and think to use your brain.

9. Spend time with family members and friends.

10. Relax.

Lesson 11 Review

Health Questions

1. What are four ways to help your bones grow and become strong? **page 69**

2. What are four ways to help your muscles grow and become strong? **page 70**

3. What are ten habits that help you grow up healthy? **page 73**

Older and Wiser

Life Skill

- **I will learn ways people age.**

To **age** is to grow older. You are getting older. Someday you will be the age your grandparents are right now. Most older people are healthy. They enjoy doing many of the things you do.

What You Will Be Able to Do

- Tell the special needs of older people.
- Tell ways you can help older people who have special needs.

Words You Will Learn

- To **age** is to grow older.

- A **handicapped ramp** is a path that makes it easier for people who have special needs to go up and down.

- A **handicapped space** is a parking place for the car or van in which a person who has special needs rides.

What Are the Special Needs of Older People?

Some older people need special health care. They might need help to live in a healthful way. They might need help hearing.

Some older people need special equipment. They might use a walker. A walker is a support to help a person walk. Some older people use a wheelchair to move about.

Some older people use an electric cart. An electric cart is a cart in which a person who has a hard time walking rides. Many stores have them.

What Are Ways I Can Help Older People Who Have Special Needs?

Be a friend to older people who have special needs. Sit and talk with your grandparents and other older people you know. Listen to what older people say.

Offer to help older people who have special needs. For example, you might carry bags of food from the store. You might push a wheelchair.

Do not play on a handicapped ramp or put your bike in a handicapped space. A **handicapped ramp** is a path that makes it easier for people who have special needs to go up and down. A **handicapped space** is a parking place for the car or van in which a person who has special needs rides.

Handicapped Symbol

Draw the Sign for a Handicapped Space

What You Will Need: Poster paper, markers, paint or crayons

1. **Copy the sign for a handicapped space on poster paper.**

2. **Write the following words on your poster.**

Lesson 12 Review

Health Questions

1. What are two special needs of some older people? **page 75**

2. What are three ways you can help older people who have special needs? **page 76**

Different and Alike

Life Skills

- I will act in ways that show I am special.
- I will work on ways to learn.

All people learn. To **learn** is to get to know about something. People learn in different ways.

What You Will Be Able to Do

- Tell ways you use your left brain and right brain.
- Tell ways to build the left brain and right brain.
- Tell ways to get help learning.

Words You Will Learn

- To **learn** is to get to know about something.

- **Memory** is being able to remember things.

- A **tutor** is a person who gives extra help to some children.

What Are Ways I Use My Left Brain and My Right Brain?

Your brain tells your body what to do. Your brain stores what you learn. Your brain has two parts. The two parts are called the left brain and the right brain.

Right brain ___ Left brain

Ways You Use Your Left Brain

You use your left brain when you do math. You use it when you spell and read. You use it for memory. **Memory** is being able to remember things.

Ways You Use Your Right Brain

You use your right brain when you draw and paint. You use it when you sing. You use it when you show feelings. You use it when you write stories.

My Health Plan

Use the same life skill.
Make your own Health Plan.

Use Your Brain

 **Life Skill**

I will work on ways to learn.

Name _____

Date _____

My Plan: I will work on ways to learn.

- **Read a library book.**
- **Count the number of crayons you have.**
- **Write your name, address, and phone number.**
- **Tell how to turn on your computer.**

- **Mold something out of clay.**
- **Draw a picture.**
- **Make a painting.**
- **Play the piano.**
- **Sing a song.**
- **Write a story.**

What I Did: I will draw the brain on a sheet of paper. My drawing will show the left brain and the right brain. I will write a way to make my left brain strong. Then I will color the left brain with a crayon. I will write a way to make my right brain strong. Then I will color the right brain with a different crayon.

How Can I Get Help with Learning?

Some children learn more easily than others. Other children have a harder time. Suppose you need help learning.

You might get a tutor. A tutor is a person who gives extra help to some children. A tutor might help with reading or numbers.

You might be in special classes. These classes make it easier for you to learn.

Lesson
13
Review

Health Questions

1. What are ways you use your left brain and right brain? **page 79**

2. What are ways to build your left brain and right brain? **page 80**

3. What are two ways you can get help with learning? **page 81**

Health Questions

1. What are three ways to take care of your lungs? **Lesson 10 page 61**

2. What are five ways to protect your brain and nerves? **Lesson 10 page 66**

3. What are four ways to help your bones grow and become strong? **Lesson 11 page 69**

4. What are three ways you can help older people who have special needs? **Lesson 12 page 76**

5. What are ways to build your left brain and right brain? **Lesson 13 page 80**

Guidelines for Making Responsible Decisions™

You work on a model airplane with a friend. You glue the pieces together. Your friend says you can sniff glue to feel happy. **Answer the questions in bold.**

1. **Is it healthful to sniff glue?**

2. **Is it safe to sniff glue?**

3. **Do you follow rules and laws if you sniff glue?**

4. **Do you show respect for yourself if you sniff glue?**

5. **Do you follow your family's guidelines if you sniff glue?**

6. **Do you show good character if you sniff glue?**

What is the responsible decision?

Health Words

Number a sheet of paper from 1–5. Write the word that belongs in the blank. Use the health words in the box.

heart
habit
handicapped ramp
learn
memory

1. A _____ _____ is a path that makes it easier for people who have special needs to go up and down. **Lesson 12**

2. _____ is being able to remember things. **Lesson 13**

3. A _____ is the way you do something most of the time. **Lesson 11**

4. Your _____ is a body part that pumps blood. **Lesson 10**

5. To _____ is to get to know about something. **Lesson 13**

Health Skills

Express Yourself

Make a poster. Draw a picture of a habit. The habit should help you grow up healthy.

Learn on Your Own

Put together the pieces of a hard puzzle. You build your right brain.

Use Thinking Skills

The heart is a muscle. Why will your heart get bigger if you exercise a lot?

Be a Good Citizen

Tell your parent or guardian a place where you have seen a handicapped ramp. Do not play on it.

Nutrition

Lesson 14
Use the Food Guide Pyramid

Lesson 15
Snack Attack

Lesson 16
Watch That Fat

Lesson 17
Germs in Food

PRACTICE

HEALTH STANDARD 4

Think About Why You Do What You Do

Practice this standard at the end of this unit.

1. **Name people and things that teach you to do things.**
   Cut out an ad for a snack from a magazine.

2. **Tell which ones help health. Tell which ones harm health.** Tell if the snack in the ad is healthful.

3. **Choose what helps your health.** Write YES on the ad if the snack is healthful.

4. **Avoid what harms health.** Throw away the ad if the snack is not healthful.

Use the Food Guide Pyramid

Life Skills

- **I will use the Food Guide Pyramid.**
- **I will follow the Dietary Guidelines.**

Your **diet** is the foods you usually eat. You can have a healthful diet. You can choose foods from the healthful food groups. A **food group** is foods that are alike.

What You Will Be Able to Do

- Tell how to use the Food Guide Pyramid.
- List the five healthful food groups.
- Tell why you should follow each of the Dietary Guidelines.

Words You Will Learn

- Your **diet** is the foods you usually eat.

- A **food group** is foods that are alike.

- The **Food Guide Pyramid** is a guide that tells how many servings you need from each food group each day.

- The **Dietary Guidelines** are guidelines for eating to help you stay healthy.

My Health Plan

Use the same life skill. Make your own Health Plan.

Eat Breakfast

Life Skill

I will use the Food Guide Pyramid.

Name_____

Date_____

My Plan: Breakfast is the meal I eat after I wake up. A healthful breakfast has foods that give me energy. A healthful breakfast has foods from the five healthful food groups. The five healthful food groups appear on page 89. These are some foods I can choose.

- Cereal
- Skim milk
- Fruit
- Rice
- Oatmeal

- Whole wheat bagel or toast
- Tuna
- English muffin
- Eggs

- Grits
- Low-fat yogurt
- Juice
- Peanut butter sandwich

What I Did: I will write the foods I eat for breakfast for the next two days.

Food Group	Monday	Tuesday
Bread	bagel	
Vegetable		
Fruit	apple	
Meat		

How Can I Use the Food Guide Pyramid?

The **Food Guide Pyramid** is a guide that tells how many servings you need from each food group each day.

Use the Food Guide Pyramid to plan meals with foods from each of the five food groups. The "Fats, Oils, and Sweets" tip of the pyramid is not a food group. Eat very few of these foods.

Use the Food Guide Pyramid to get the correct number of servings from each food group each day.

The Food Guide Pyramid

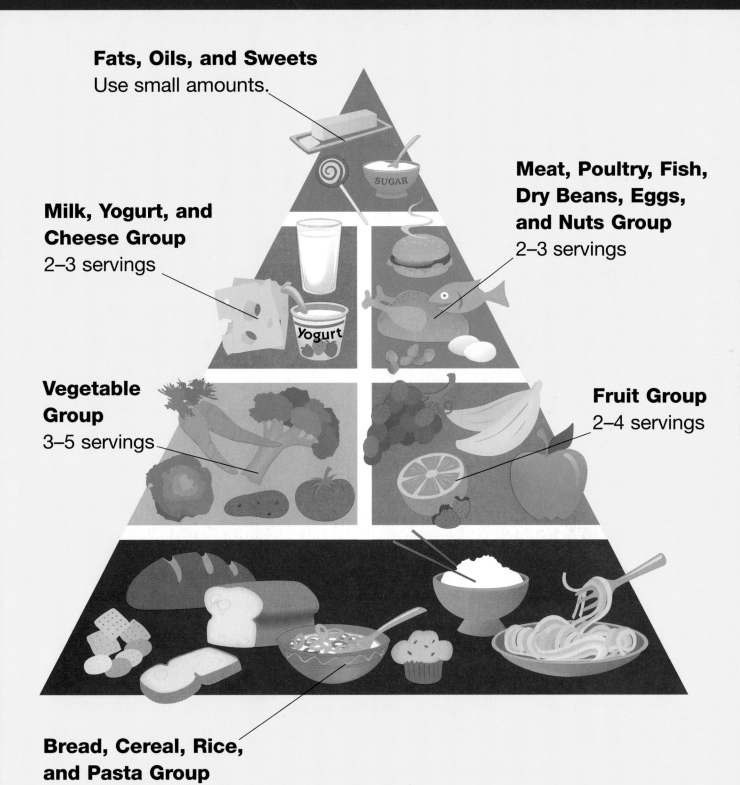

Fats, Oils, and Sweets
Use small amounts.

Meat, Poultry, Fish, Dry Beans, Eggs, and Nuts Group
2–3 servings

Milk, Yogurt, and Cheese Group
2–3 servings

Vegetable Group
3–5 servings

Fruit Group
2–4 servings

Bread, Cereal, Rice, and Pasta Group
6–11 servings

How Can I Use the Dietary Guidelines?

These **Dietary Guidelines** are guidelines for eating to help you stay healthy.

1. **Stay at a healthful weight.** A healthful weight helps you have a healthy heart. It keeps your blood vessels healthy.

2. **Get plenty of exercise.** Exercise helps you stay at a healthful weight. It makes your heart muscle strong.

3. **Follow the Food Guide Pyramid.** You will get the servings you need from each food group each day.

4. **Eat plenty of grains.** They help you have a daily bowel movement. This helps prevent cancer.

5. **Eat fruits and vegetables**. They help protect against heart disease and some cancers. They also help you have a daily bowel movement.

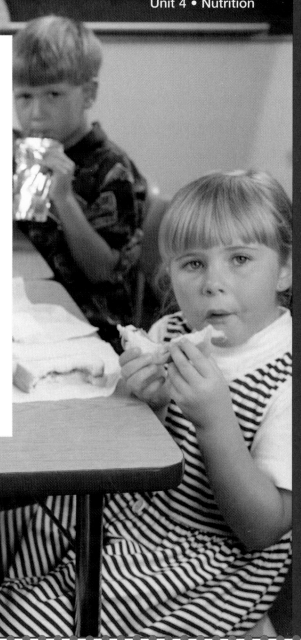

6. **Keep foods safe**. Wash, store, and cook food in the right way. This keeps germs out of food.

7. **Avoid fatty foods.** This helps prevent heart disease.

8. **Cut down on sugars.** Too much sugar can cause cavities.

9. **Go easy on salt.** Too much salt might harm your blood vessels.

10. **Do not drink alcohol.** Alcohol harms your brain, heart, and liver.

Lesson 14

Review

Health Questions

1. What are two ways you can use the Food Guide Pyramid? **page 88**

2. What are the five healthful food groups? **page 89**

3. What is the reason you should follow each one of the Dietary Guidelines? **pages 90-91**

Snack Attack

Life Skills

- **I will eat healthful meals and snacks.**
- **I will choose healthful fast foods.**

A **snack** is a food or drink you have between meals. Choose healthful meals and snacks. Use the Dietary Guidelines to choose meals and snacks. The **Dietary Guidelines** are guidelines for eating to help you stay healthy.

What You Will Be Able to Do

- Tell how to choose healthful snacks.
- Tell how to choose healthful fast foods.

Words You Will Learn

- A **snack** is a food or drink you have between meals.

- The **Dietary Guidelines** are guidelines for eating to help you stay healthy.

- A **fast food restaurant** is a restaurant that serves food quickly.

How Can I Choose Healthful Snacks?

Use the Dietary Guidelines to choose healthful snacks. Follow the Food Guide Pyramid.

Choose snacks that help you stay at a healthful weight.

Choose fruits and vegetables for snacks.

Choose grains for snacks.

Choose few snacks with sugar.

Choose few fatty snacks.

Choose few salty snacks.

How Can I Choose Healthful Fast Foods?

A **fast food restaurant** is a restaurant that serves food quickly.

Use the Dietary Guidelines to choose healthful fast foods.

Choose fast foods that help you stay at a healthful weight.

Small or junior burger

Salad with low-fat dressing

Choose grains.

Whole-wheat bun

Choose fruits and vegetables.

Veggie pizza

Yogurt with fresh fruit

Choose few fatty foods.

Low-fat milkshake

Choose few fast foods with sugar.

Orange juice

Choose few salty foods.

Baked potato with no added salt.

Caffeine Hunt

1. **Read the box below.**

2. **Go to a grocery store with your parents or guardian.** Find three foods or drinks that have caffeine in them. Write them down.

3. **Share your list with your classmates.**

Caffeine

Some foods and drinks have caffeine. Too much caffeine can make you jumpy. It can keep you awake when you want to sleep. Limit how much caffeine you eat or drink.

Activity

Lesson
15
Review

Health Questions

1. How can you choose healthful snacks? **page 93**

2. How can you choose healthful fast foods? **page 94**

Watch That Fat

Life Skills

- **I will stay at a healthful weight.**
- **I will read food labels.**

Children your age weigh different amounts. Your doctor will tell you what you should weigh. A **healthful weight** is the weight that keeps you in good health.

What You Will Be Able to Do

- Tell ways to keep from being overfat.
- Tell how to read a food label.

Words You Will Learn

- A **healthful weight** is the weight that keeps you in good health.

- **Overfat** is having too much body fat.

- A **food label** is the label on a food container that shows facts about the food.

How Can I Keep from Being Overfat?

Overfat is having too much body fat. Here are three ways to keep from being overfat.

Limit TV and computer time.
Spend less than two hours each day. You do not exercise when you watch TV or play on a computer. You are more likely to snack.

Exercise or play outdoors.
Ride your bike. Play kickball. Join a soccer or softball team.

Eat healthful foods.
Follow the Dietary Guidelines. Choose snacks that are low in fat and sugar.

What's on a Food Label?

Activity

What You Will Need: Empty food box

A **food label** is the label on a food container that shows facts about the food. You can read food labels to help you choose healthful foods.

Total Fat
A food label shows how much fat is in the food.

Food Label for Peanut Butter

Nutrition Facts	Amount/Serving	%DV*	Amount/Serving	%DV*
Serving Size 2 Tbsp. (35g)	**Total Fat** 12g	**18**%	**Total Carb.** 15g	**5**%
Servings Per Container about 14	Sat Fat 2.5g	**12**%	Dietary Fiber 2g	**8**%
	Cholest. 0mg	**0**%	Sugars 4g	
Calories 190	**Sodium** 220mg	**9**%	**Protein** 8g	
Fat Cal. 110	Iron 4% • Niacin 25% • Vitamin B₆ 6% • Folic Acid 6%			
*Percent Daily Values (DV) are based on a 2,000 calorie diet.	Magnesium 15% • Zinc 6% • Copper 10%			
	Not a significant source of vitamin A, vitamin C, and calcium.			

Sugars
A food label shows how much sugar is in the food.

1. **Bring an empty food box from home.** The food box should have a food label on it.

2. **Hold up the food box.** Tell your class how much total fat is in the food. Tell how much sugar is in the food.

TV Ad Jingles

Activity

1. **Sing a food jingle you have heard on TV.** A jingle is a catchy tune to get you to remember something.

2. **Have your class guess which food you are singing about.**

3. **Tell whether the food has lots of fat or sugars in it.** Why does the company want you to remember the jingle?

Lesson 16

Review

Health Questions

1. What are three ways you can keep from being overfat? **page 97**

2. What are two facts you can learn from reading a food label? **page 98**

Germs in Food

Life Skills

- **I will protect myself from germs in food.**
- **I will use good table manners.**

Germs are tiny living things that can make you sick. Germs can get into food. You can get sick when you eat the food. Protect yourself from germs in food.

What You Will Be Able to Do

- Tell ways to keep germs out of food.

- Tell reasons to use good table manners.

Words You Will Learn

- **Germs** are tiny living things that can make you sick.

- **Good table manners** are polite ways to eat.

How Can I Keep Germs Out of Food?

Wash your hands with soap and water. Wash before you set the table. Wash before you prepare food or eat.

Do not eat or drink after someone else. Do not share a soda pop or ice cream cone.

Do not eat food that you have dropped on the ground. Suppose you drop a sucker. Is it okay to just rinse it off? NO! The sucker still might have germs.

Do not share silverware, straws, or cups.

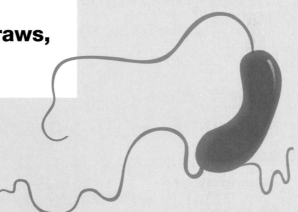

Germs are tiny living things that can make you sick.

How Can I Have Good Table Manners?

Good table manners are polite ways to eat.

Wash your hands before you eat.

You will not get germs in your food.

Chew with your mouth closed.

No one wants to see the food you are chewing.

Do not talk with your mouth full.

Other people cannot tell what you are saying.

Do not reach across the table.

Ask someone to pass you what you want.

Do not grab food off someone else's plate.

Get your own food from the serving dish.

Use... Guidelines for Making Responsible Decisions™

Situation:

Your friend got a bubble gum ice cream cone. You got a chocolate ice cream cone. Your friend says, "I want a lick of your ice cream."

Lesson 17 Review

Response:

Answer the questions in bold.

1. **Is it healthful to share your ice cream cone?**

2. Is it safe to share your ice cream cone?

3. **Do you follow rules and laws if you share your ice cream cone?**

4. **Do you show respect for yourself if you share your ice cream cone?**

5. **Do you follow your family's guidelines if you share your ice cream cone?**

6. Do you show good character if you share your ice cream cone?

What is the responsible decision?

Health Questions

1. What are four ways you can keep germs out of food? **page 101**

2. What are five good table manners? **page 102**

Review

Health Questions

1. What are two ways you can use the Food Guide Pyramid? **Lesson 14 page 88**

2. How can you use the Dietary Guidelines to choose healthful snacks? **Lesson 15 page 93**

3. What are three ways you can keep from being overfat? **Lesson 16 page 97**

4. What are four ways you can keep germs out of food? **Lesson 17 page 101**

5. What are five good table manners? **Lesson 17 page 102**

Guidelines for Making Responsible Decisions™

Your cousin wants to spend hours playing computer games with you. **Answer the questions in bold.**

1. **Is it healthful to spend hours playing computer games?**

2. Is it safe to spend hours playing computer games?

3. **Do you follow rules and laws if you spend hours playing computer games?**

4. **Do you show respect for yourself if you spend hours playing computer games?**

5. **Do you follow your family's guidelines if you spend hours playing computer games?**

6. Do you show good character if you spend hours playing computer games?

What is the responsible decision?

Health Words

Number a sheet of paper from 1–5. Write the word that belongs in the blank. Use the health words in the box.

> **diet**
>
> **Food Guide Pyramid**
>
> **germs**
>
> **overfat**
>
> **snack**

1. _____ are tiny living things that can make you sick. **Lesson 17**

2. Your _____ is the foods you usually eat. **Lesson 14**

3. A _____ is a food or drink you have between meals. **Lesson 15**

4. _____ is having too much body fat. **Lesson 16**

5. The _____ _____ _____ is a guide that tells how many servings you need from each food group each day. **Lesson 14**

Health Skills

Express Yourself

Prepare a skit that shows good table manners. Ask a friend to help. Perform the skit for your class.

Learn on Your Own

Visit a fast food restaurant with your parents or guardian. Ask for a guide that shows how much fat is in each food. Write three low-fat foods.

Use Thinking Skills

How can reading a food label help you follow the Dietary Guidelines?

Be a Good Citizen

Plan three healthful meals for your family. Plan a breakfast, a lunch, and a dinner. Use the Food Guide Pyramid.

Unit 5

Personal Health and Physical Activity

Lesson 18
Check Me Out

Lesson 19
Don't Forget to Brush and Floss

Lesson 20
Look Sharp

Lesson 21
Exercise and Get Fit

Lesson 22
Exercise in Safe Ways

PRACTICE

HEALTH STANDARD 3 **Make Health Plans**

Practice this standard at the end of this unit.

1. Write the life skill you want to practice.
I will get plenty of exercise.

2. Give a plan for what you will do. Look at
pages 124–125. Tell exercises you can do for heart
fitness this week.

3. Keep track of what you do. Draw a star on
your plan each day you do an exercise.

4. Tell how your plan worked. Count your stars
at the end of the week. You need 3–5.

Check Me Out

Life Skills
- **I will have checkups.**
- **I will keep a health record.**

A **checkup** is a check by your doctor to learn how healthy you are. Your doctor will check your eyes and ears.

What You Will Be Able to Do

- Tell what happens during an eye checkup.
- Tell ways to protect your vision.
- Tell what happens during an ear checkup.
- Tell ways to protect hearing.
- Tell what to write in your health record.

Words You Will Learn

- A **checkup** is a check by your doctor to learn how healthy you are.

- Your **vision** is how well you see.

- A **hearing loss** is not being able to hear sounds you should hear.

- A **health record** is written information your family keeps about your health.

What Happens During an Eye Checkup?

The doctor checks to see if your eyes are healthy. The doctor shines a light into each of your eyes. The doctor can see the blood vessels in your eyes. Blood must flow easily to eyes to keep them healthy.

The doctor checks your vision. Your **vision** (VI·zhuhn) is how well you see. You cover your eyes one at a time. You read letters on a chart. The doctor finds out which letters you can see clearly. You might need glasses if you do not see clearly.

Protect Your Vision

• Have eye checkups.

• Wear sunglasses when the sun is bright.

• Do not rub your eye if something gets in it.

• Be careful when you use something sharp or pointed.

• Wear special glasses for sports.

What Happens During an Ear Checkup?

The doctor checks to see if your ears are healthy. The doctor looks inside your ears. The doctor might remove wax from your ear. Too much wax might keep you from hearing clearly.

The doctor checks your hearing. You put on something that looks like earmuffs. You raise your hand when you hear certain sounds. A **hearing loss** is not being able to hear sounds you should hear.

Some children need help with hearing. They might have a hearing aid. A hearing aid is worn in the ear to help a person hear better.

Protect Your Hearing

• Have your hearing checked.

• Do not try to clean the inside of your ears.

• Do not put anything inside your ear.

• Stay away from loud noises.

• Wear a batter's helmet when you play baseball.

Ear drum _____

Make a Health Record

What You Will Need: Paper and pencil

1. **Copy the health record in the box.** A **health record** is written information your family keeps about your health.

2. **Take your health record home.** Ask your parents or guardian to help you finish your health record.

My Health Record

Foods I Eat: _____

_____

Exercises I Like: _____

_____

Shots I Had: _____

_____

Dates I Had Checkups:

_____

Lesson 18 Review

Health Questions

1. What two things happen during an eye checkup? **page 109**

2. What are five ways to protect your vision? **page 109**

3. What two things happen during an ear checkup? **page 110**

4. What are five ways to protect your hearing? **page 110**

5. What information belongs in a health record? **page 111**

Don't Forget to Brush and Floss

Life Skill

• **I will take care of my teeth.**

Your teeth help you chew your food. They help you smile. They help you speak. Don't forget to take care of your teeth.

What You Will Be Able to Do

• Tell ways to take care of your teeth.

• Make a health plan to floss each day.

Words You Will Learn

• A **cavity** is a hole in a tooth.

• To **floss** is to remove the sticky material from teeth.

• A **mouthguard** is something worn in the mouth to protect the teeth and gums.

• A **safety belt** is a lap belt and a shoulder belt.

How Can I Take Care of My Teeth?

Brush your teeth at least two times a day. A **cavity** is a hole in a tooth. Brushing keeps you from getting a cavity.

Floss every day. To **floss** is to remove the sticky material from teeth. A thin thread is used to floss.

Have a dental checkup every six months. Your dentist helps keep your teeth healthy.

Choose healthful foods, and drink milk. Cut down on foods with sugar.

Wear a mouthguard for sports. A **mouthguard** is something worn in the mouth to protect the teeth and gums.

Wear a safety belt in a car. A **safety belt** is a lap belt and a shoulder belt.

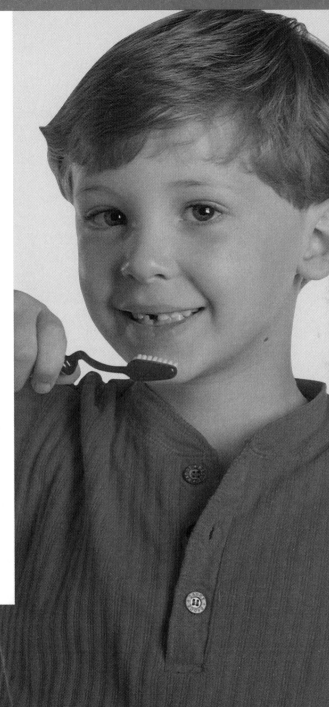

My Health Plan

Use the same life skill. Make your own Health Plan.

Floss Each Day

Life Skill

I will take care of my teeth.

Name _____

Date _____

My Plan: I will floss my teeth each day. I will use the pictures below to help me.

Step 1: Wind the floss around your middle fingers.

Step 2: Gently move the floss between your teeth.

Step 3: Move the floss upward on the bottom teeth.

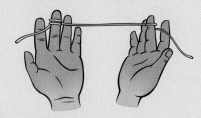

What I Did: I will put a check on my calendar each day that I flossed my teeth.

My Calendar	M	T	W	Th	F	S	S
	✓	✓	✓	✓	✓	✓	✓

My Teeth Book

What You Will Need: Construction paper, crayons, scissors, and stapler

1. **Draw and cut out six teeth.** Use one sheet of paper for each tooth.

2. **Write on the first sheet, "My Teeth Book."** Write one way to take care of your teeth on each sheet.

3. **Staple your book together.** Take it home to show your family.

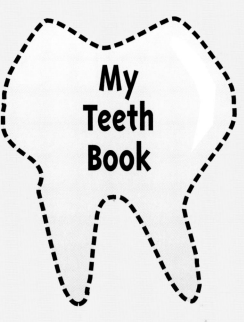

My Teeth Book

Lesson 19 Review

Health Questions

1. What are six ways to take care of your teeth? **page 113**

2. What are three steps for flossing your teeth? **page 114**

Look Sharp

Life Skills

- I will be neat and clean.
- I will get plenty of sleep and rest.

To look sharp is to look your best. Your hair and skin are clean. Your clothes are neat. You feel and look alert.

What You Will Be Able to Do

- Tell ways you can look sharp.
- Tell reasons you need sleep and rest.
- Tell ways to help you sleep.

Words You Will Learn

- **Grooming** is taking care of your body and your appearance.

- **Sleep** is a time when you are not awake.

- A **rest** is a short break from activity.

How Can I Look Sharp?

Grooming is taking care of your body and your appearance. Grooming helps you look sharp.

Keep your body clean and neat. Take a bath or shower every day. Shampoo and brush your hair often.

Keep your fingernails clean and neat. Do not bite your fingernails. Use a nail brush to get dirt from under your nails. Keep your nails short.

Keep clothes clean and neat. Hang up or fold clothes when you take them off. Wash them when they are dirty. Tell your parents or guardian if your clothes get torn.

Why Do I Need Sleep and Rest?

Sleep is a time when you are not awake. A **rest** is a short break from activity. You need sleep and rest for three reasons.

Sleep and rest help your body relax. Your heart beat slows down. You breathe slower. Your muscles do not work as hard.

Sleep and rest help you grow. Bones grow while you sleep and rest. Muscles grow while you sleep and rest.

Sleep and rest help you be alert. Sleep helps you be alert the next day. Getting rest during the day keeps you alert. Suppose you feel tired. Take a rest. You will feel more alert afterwards.

Stars in Our Classroom

What You Will Need: Construction paper, crayons, and scissors

1. **Draw and cut out a star from a sheet of construction paper.** You need sleep to be a star during the day.

2. **Look at the Ways to Help You Sleep.** Write one of the ways on your star.

3. **Have your teacher staple your star to the bulletin board.** The bulletin board will say, "Stars in Our Classroom."

Ways to Help You Sleep

- Limit caffeine.
- Read.
- Listen to soft music.
- Take a warm bath.

Activity

Lesson 20

Review

Health Questions

1. What are three things you can do to look sharp? **page 117**

2. What are three reasons you need sleep and rest? **page 118**

3. What are four ways to help you sleep? **page 119**

Exercise and Get Fit

Life Skill

• **I will get plenty of exercise.**

Exercise is moving your muscles. What exercises do you enjoy? Do you like to bike, swim, or skate?

What You Will Be Able to Do

• Explain why you need to get plenty of exercise.

• Show how to stretch muscles the correct way.

• Tell exercises that make muscles strong.

• Tell the correct way to build heart fitness.

Words You Will Learn

• **Exercise** is moving your muscles.

• **Fitness** is having your body in top form.

• A **stretch** is an exercise that helps you bend and move easily.

• **Heart fitness** is having a strong heart muscle so you do not tire easily.

Why Do I Need to Get Plenty of Exercise?

Exercise helps you do better in school. It helps blood flow to your brain. You think clearly. You do not get restless when you do schoolwork.

Exercise helps you manage stress. Stress is the way your body reacts to strong feelings. Exercise helps you relax.

Exercise helps you have fitness. **Fitness** is having your body in top form. You have energy for work and play. You do not tire easily.

What Is the Correct Way to Stretch Muscles?

A **stretch** is an exercise that helps you bend and move easily. You need to do stretches two to four days a week. Do stretches for five minutes before you do hard exercise.

How to Stretch

1. Stretch your muscles until you feel a slight pull.

2. Hold each stretch while you count to 15.

3. Count to 30 between each stretch.

4. Repeat each stretch three to five times.

What Exercises Make My Muscles Strong?

Strong muscles help you lift, pull, and push. Strong muscles help you kick and throw. Do exercises for the different muscles in your body.

Riding your bike makes leg muscles strong.

Climbing makes arm muscles strong.

What Is the Correct Way to Build Heart Fitness?

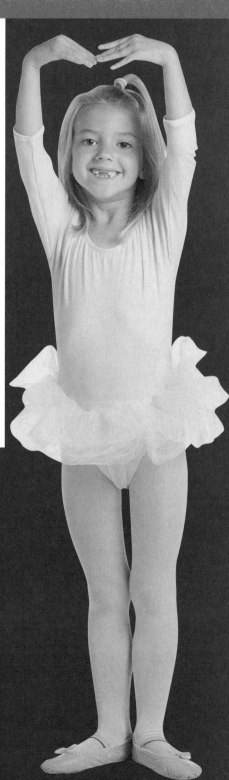

Heart fitness is having a strong heart muscle so you do not tire easily. You need to do exercises for heart fitness three to five days a week.

How to Build Heart Fitness

1. Stretch first.

2. Start slow.

3. Get your heart rate up.

4. Keep a steady pace for 15 to 20 minutes.

5. Slow down.

Dancing

Running

Jumping

Try different exercises to build heart fitness.

Jumping Rope

Ice Skating

Biking

Skiing

In-line Skating

Hiking

Swimming

Playing Soccer

Walking

Skateboarding

Practice for the President's Challenge

Activity

1. **Practice for the test.** *The President's Challenge* is a fitness test for boys and girls ages 6 to 17. There are five tests. Your teacher can help you practice.

2. **Take the test.** Your teacher will tell you how well you did.

Curl-ups test how strong the muscles below your stomach are.

One-mile walk or run tests how strong the muscles in your legs are. It tests heart fitness.

Shuttle run tests how strong the muscles in your legs are. It tests heart fitness.

Pull-ups test how strong the muscles in your arms and shoulders are.

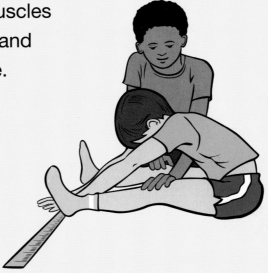

V-sit and reach tests how easily the muscles in your legs and back can stretch.

Lesson 21

Review

Health Questions

1. What are three reasons you need to get plenty of exercise? **page 121**

2. What is the correct way to stretch muscles? **page 122**

3. What are three exercises that make muscles strong? **page 123**

4. What is the correct way to build heart fitness? **page 124**

Exercise in Safe Ways

Life Skills

- **I will exercise in safe ways.**
- **I will follow safety rules for sports and games.**

Exercise is fun. But you can get hurt when you exercise. Exercise in safe ways. Then you will not get hurt.

What You Will Be Able to Do

- Tell safe ways to exercise.
- Tell how to be a good sport.

Words You Will Learn

- A **warm-up** is easy activity before you exercise.

- A **cool-down** is easy activity after you exercise.

- To **cooperate** is to work together.

How Can I Exercise in Safe Ways?

Do a warm-up. A **warm-up** is easy activity before you exercise. A warm-up gets your muscles ready for exercise. Walk or jog for three to five minutes. To jog is to run slowly. Stretch your muscles.

Wear the correct gear.
Wear running shoes when you run. Wear a helmet when you bike. Wear pads to protect your wrists, knees, and elbows when you skate.

Do a cool-down. A **cool-down** is easy activity after you exercise. A cool-down helps your heart rate slow down. A cool-down helps your muscles stay loose. They do not cramp. Walk or jog for five to ten minutes after exercise. Stretch your muscles.

How Can I Be a Good Sport?

Follow rules for sports and games. Learn the rules of the game or sport. Take your turn. Do not cheat. Follow safety rules. Be careful with bats, balls, and hockey sticks.

Use good manners.
Do not hog equipment, like swings. Let others have a turn. Pass on the left when you bike on a bike path. Do not yell at other players unless it is part of the game. Do not use put-downs.

Cooperate with your team. To **cooperate** (koh·AH·puh·rayt) is to work together. Do your best. Do not brag about yourself. Praise others on your team. Do not put them down when they make mistakes. Help them when they need help.

Use... Guidelines for Making Responsible Decisions™

Situation:

You and a friend are playing on a seesaw. Two other children want a turn. Your friend does not want to get off.

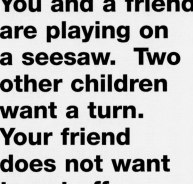

Response:

Answer the questions in bold.

1. Is it healthful to hog the seesaw?

2. Is it safe to hog the seesaw?

3. **Do you follow rules and laws if you hog the seesaw?**

4. **Do you show respect for yourself if you hog the seesaw?**

5. **Do you follow your family's guidelines if you hog the seesaw?**

6. **Do you show good character if you hog the seesaw?**

What is the responsible decision?

Lesson
22

Review

Health Questions

1. What are three safe ways to exercise? **page 129**

2. What are three ways to be a good sport? **page 130**

Health Questions

1. What two things happen during an ear checkup? **Lesson 18 page 110**

2. What are three steps for flossing your teeth? **Lesson 19 page 114**

3. What are three things you can do to look sharp? **Lesson 20 page 117**

4. What are three exercises that make muscles strong? **Lesson 21 page 123**

5. What are three ways to be a good sport? **Lesson 22 page 130**

Guidelines for Making Responsible Decisions™

You want to go to bed right away. You have not brushed and flossed your teeth. **Answer the questions in bold.**

1. **Is it healthful not to brush and floss your teeth?**

2. Is it safe not to brush and floss your teeth?

3. Do you follow rules and laws if you do not brush and floss your teeth?

4. **Do you show respect for yourself if you do not brush and floss your teeth?**

5. **Do you follow your family's guidelines if you do not brush and floss your teeth?**

6. Do you show good character if you do not brush and floss your teeth?

What is the responsible decision?

Health Words

Number a sheet of paper from 1–5. Write the word that belongs in the blank. Use the health words in the box.

> **exercise**
>
> **floss**
>
> **checkup**
>
> **rest**
>
> **warm-up**

1. To _____ is to remove the sticky material from teeth. **Lesson 19**

2. _____ is moving your muscles. **Lesson 21**

3. A _____ is a check by your doctor to learn how healthy you are. **Lesson 18**

4. A _____ is easy activity before you exercise. **Lesson 22**

5. A _____ is a short break from activity. **Lesson 20**

Health Skills

Express Yourself

Draw and cut out a large pair of sunglasses. Write two ways to protect your vision on the sunglasses.

Learn on Your Own

Find a book or magazine about a sport or game. Find out what gear to wear to play the sport or game safely.

Use Thinking Skills

Suppose you do not get enough sleep one night. Why might you do poorly in school the next day?

Be a Good Citizen

Ask your health or physical education teacher to show you some stretches. Teach them to your family.

Unit
6

Say
NO!

Alcohol, Tobacco, and Other Drugs

Medicine Safety

Life Skill

- **I will use medicine in safe ways.**

A **drug** is something that changes the way your mind or body works. A **medicine** is a drug used to treat an illness or injury. You need to know safe ways to use medicine.

What You Will Be Able to Do

- Tell times when you need medicine.
- List rules for using medicine in safe ways.

Words You Will Learn

- A **drug** is something that changes the way your mind or body works.

- A **medicine** is a drug used to treat an illness or injury.

- A **disease** is an illness.

- A **side effect** is an unwanted feeling or illness after taking a medicine.

Lesson 23
Medicine Safety

Lesson 24
Alcohol...No Way!

Lesson 25
Tobacco...No Way!

Lesson 26
Drug-Free Pledge

PRACTICE
HEALTH STANDARD 6 | **Make Responsible Decisions**

You are at a friend's house and feel sick. The friend says, "Take my medicine."

1. **Tell what the choices are.** You could take the medicine. You could say NO.

2. **Use Guidelines for Making Responsible Decisions.™**
   - **Is it healthful to take medicine from a friend?**
   - **Is it safe to take medicine from a friend?**
   - Do I follow rules and laws if…?
   - Do I show respect for myself and others if…?
   - **Do I follow my family's guidelines if I take the medicine?**
   - Do I show good character if...?

3. **Tell what the responsible decision is.**

4. **Tell what happens if you make this decision.**

When Do I Need Medicine?

You might need medicine when you are sick. Your parents or guardian might give you medicine for a cold.

You might need medicine when you are hurt. Your parents or guardian might put medicine on a cut.

You might need medicine to keep from getting a disease. A disease (di·ZEEZ) is an illness. Your doctor might give you a shot to keep you from getting chickenpox.

What Are Rules for Using Medicine in Safe Ways?

Take medicine only from a trusted adult. A trusted adult is your parent, guardian, or a person who has his or her permission. A trusted adult is a doctor or nurse.

Do not take medicine that belongs to someone else. Your body size and weight are not the same as someone else's.

Tell your parent or guardian if you have a side effect after taking a medicine. A side effect is an unwanted feeling or illness after taking a medicine. Suppose you feel dizzy after taking medicine. Feeling dizzy is a side effect. Your parent or guardian will call your doctor.

The Medicine Cabinet

What You Will Need: Construction paper, scissors, crayons, and tape

1. **Draw an outline of a medicine bottle on construction paper.** Print the word "Medicine" on the bottle. Cut out the medicine bottle.

2. **Tell one of the rules for the safe use of medicine.**

3. **Your teacher will put a medicine cabinet made of paper on the wall.** Use tape to place your bottle in the medicine cabinet.

Lesson 23 Review

Health Questions

1. What are three times you might need medicine? **page 137**

2. What are three rules for using medicine in safe ways? **page 138**

Alcohol... No Way!

Life Skills

- I will not drink alcohol.
- I will tell ways people who use harmful drugs can get help.

Alcohol is a drug found in some drinks that slows down the body. It is harmful for you to drink alcohol.

What You Will Be Able to Do

- Tell ways alcohol harms your health.
- Tell people to talk to if someone you know is a problem drinker.

Words You Will Learn

- **Alcohol** is a drug found in some drinks that slows down the body.

- **Cancer** is a disease in which harmful cells grow.

- A **problem drinker** is an adult who drinks too much and has wrong actions.

How Can Alcohol Harm My Health?

Alcohol keeps you from thinking clearly. You will make wrong decisions. You will not remember things. You will do poorly in school.

Alcohol slows down movement. You will not walk straight. You can fall. You can have an accident.

Alcohol can cause disease. Alcohol destroys your liver cells. Alcohol kills brain cells. Alcohol can change healthy cells. Drinking alcohol can cause cancer. **Cancer** (KAN·ser) is a disease in which harmful cells grow. Drinking alcohol can cause heart disease.

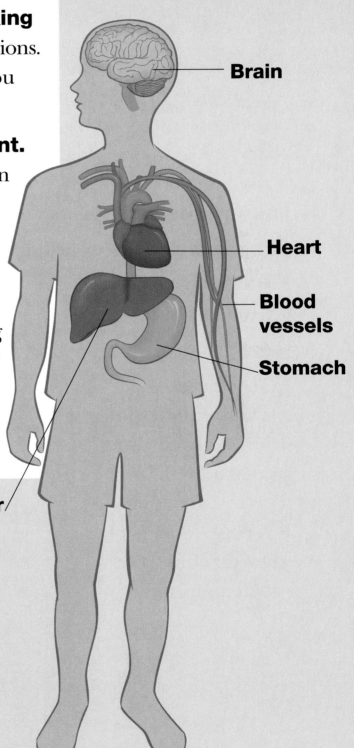

Brain

Heart

Blood vessels

Stomach

Liver

Drinking alcohol can harm different body parts.

What People Can I Talk to If Someone I Know Is a Problem Drinker?

A **problem drinker** is an adult who drinks too much and has wrong actions. Talk to a trusted adult if you know an adult who is a problem drinker.

- **Your parents or guardian**
- **Your school nurse**
- **Your school counselor**
- **Your doctor**

The trusted adult can get help for the problem drinker. The trusted adult can help you feel less sad and afraid. It is never your fault when an adult is a problem drinker.

Use... Guidelines for Making Responsible Decisions™

Situation:

Someone offers you a sip of beer. What should you do?

Response:

Answer the questions in bold.

1. **Is it healthful to take a sip of beer?**

2. **Is it safe to take a sip of beer?**

3. **Do you follow rules and laws if you take a sip of beer?**

4. **Do you show respect for yourself if you take a sip of beer?**

5. **Do you follow your family's guidelines if you take a sip of beer?**

6. **Do you show good character if you take a sip of beer?**

What is the responsible decision?

Lesson 24

Review

Health Questions

1. What are three ways alcohol can harm your health? **page 141**

2. Who are four people you can talk to if someone you know is a problem drinker? **page 142**

Lesson 25

Tobacco... No Way!

**Life Skills**

- **I will not use tobacco.**
- **I will stay away from secondhand smoke.**

Tobacco is a plant that has harmful drugs in it. Chewing or smoking tobacco harms health. Breathing tobacco smoke harms health.

What You Will Be Able to Do

- Tell ways tobacco harms your health.
- Tell how you can stay away from secondhand smoke.

Words You Will Learn

- **Nicotine** is a harmful drug found in tobacco.
- **Smokeless tobacco** is tobacco that is chewed.
- **Addiction** is letting a drug control you.
- **Secondhand smoke** is smoke from other people's cigarettes and cigars.

How Can Tobacco Harm My Health?

Tobacco harms your heart and blood vessels. Nicotine (NI·kuh·teen) is a harmful drug found in tobacco. Nicotine makes the heart work harder. It makes blood vessels narrow. The heart gets less blood and oxygen.

Tobacco harms your lungs. You will have a hard time breathing if you smoke. You will tire easily.

Tobacco harms your teeth and gums. Smokeless tobacco is tobacco that is chewed. It can make your gums swell. It can make your teeth fall out.

Tobacco can cause addiction. Addiction is letting a drug control you. It is hard to stop using tobacco.

Don't Start!

You can get addicted to tobacco if you smoke just one cigarette. You can get addicted if you chew smokeless tobacco just one time. The younger you are, the more likely you are to get addicted!

How Can I Stay Away from Secondhand Smoke?

Secondhand smoke is smoke from other people's cigarettes and cigars. Secondhand smoke can harm your heart and lungs. It can cause you to cough and sneeze. It can cause your eyes to sting.

Do not be around people who are smoking. Ask people not to smoke. Say, "Would you please not smoke? Smoke stings my eyes."

Eat in restaurants where smoking is not allowed. Sit in the non-smoking section if smoking is allowed.

Talk to your parents or guardian about having a "no smoking" rule in your home.

Suppose you are in a room where other people are smoking. You breathe secondhand smoke for one hour. This is the same as smoking 25 cigarettes.

Use...

Guidelines for Making Responsible Decisions™

Situation:

Your friend's aunt lights a cigarette. Your friend's parents allow people to smoke in their home. They say it cannot harm you to breathe secondhand smoke for one evening.

Response:

Answer the questions in bold.

1. **Is it healthful to breathe secondhand smoke?**

2. Is it safe to breathe secondhand smoke?

3. Do you follow rules and laws if you breathe secondhand smoke?

4. **Do you show respect for yourself if you breathe secondhand smoke?**

5. **Do you follow your family's guidelines if you breathe secondhand smoke?**

6. Do you show good character if you breathe secondhand smoke?

What is the responsible decision?

Lesson 25

Review

Health Questions

1. What are four ways tobacco harms your health? **page 145**

2. What are three ways you can stay away from secondhand smoke? **page 146**

Drug-Free Pledge

Life Skill

- **I will not use drugs that are against the law.**

It is against the law to use some drugs. They harm the mind and body. Pledge to stay away from these drugs.

What You Will Be Able to Do

- Explain reasons you should be drug-free.
- Tell ways you can say NO to drugs.
- List drugs that are against the law.

Words You Will Learn

- To be **drug-free** is...

  ...to say NO to drugs that are against the law,

  ...to stay away from people who use drugs in wrong ways, and

  ...to stay away from parties where people are using drugs in wrong ways.

- **Say NO skills** are ways to say NO to wrong decisions.

Why Should I Be Drug-Free?

To be **drug-free** is:

- to say NO to drugs that are against the law,

- to stay away from people who use drugs in wrong ways, and

- to stay away from parties where people are using drugs in wrong ways.

These children give reasons you should be drug-free.

I want to be healthy. I harm my mind and body if I use drugs.

I want to show good character. It is wrong to use drugs.

I want to follow my family's guidelines. My parents or guardians do not want me to use drugs.

I want to follow rules and laws. I break the law if I use drugs. I break school rules if I use drugs.

I want to be safe. I will have accidents if I use drugs.

I want to show respect for myself and others. I care about my health. I care about my family and friends.

Say NO to Drugs

Activity

1. **Pair up with a classmate.** Pretend you have been offered a drug.

2. **Practice say NO skills.** Say NO skills are ways to say NO to wrong decisions. Use the say NO skills in the box.

Say NO Skills

1. **Look directly at the person who offers you a harmful drug.**

2. **Say, "NO, I will not use harmful drugs."**

3. **Tell why you are saying NO.** Give one of the reasons on page 149.

4. **Repeat your NO if you need to.** Say again, "NO, I will not use harmful drugs."

5. **Do not change your mind about using harmful drugs.** Shake your head, say, "No," and walk away.

What Are Drugs That Are Against the Law?

Marijuana (mehr·uh·WAH·nuh) is a drug that is against the law. Marijuana harms memory. It makes it hard to pay attention.

Cocaine (koh·KAYN) is a drug that is against the law. Cocaine speeds up the body. It can make your heart stop working.

Crack is a drug that is against the law. Crack is a form of cocaine. It speeds up the body.

Ecstasy is a drug that is against the law. Ecstasy harms the brain. It can harm the way a person thinks.

I will not use drugs that are against the law.

Lesson 26
Review

Health Questions

1. What are six reasons to be drug-free? **page 149**

2. What are five say NO skills you can use if someone offers you a harmful drug? **page 150**

3. What are four drugs that are against the law? **page 151**

Health Questions

1. What are three rules for using medicine in safe ways? **Lesson 23 page 138**

2. What are three ways alcohol can harm your health? **Lesson 24 page 141**

3. What are three ways you can stay away from secondhand smoke? **Lesson 25 page 146**

4. What are six reasons to be drug-free? **Lesson 26 page 149**

5. What are five say NO skills you can use if someone offers you a harmful drug? **Lesson 25 page 150**

Guidelines for Making Responsible Decisions™

Someone offers you chewing tobacco. What should you do? **Answer the questions in bold.**

1. **Is it healthful to chew tobacco?**

2. **Is it safe to chew tobacco?**

3. **Do you follow rules and laws if you chew tobacco?**

4. **Do you show respect for yourself if you chew tobacco?**

5. **Do you follow your family's guidelines if you chew tobacco?**

6. **Do you show good character if you chew tobacco?**

What is the responsible decision?

Health Words

Number a sheet of paper from 1–5. Write the word that belongs in the blank. Use the health words in the box.

> **addiction**
>
> **say NO skills**
>
> **medicine**
>
> **problem drinker**
>
> **secondhand smoke**

1. _____ _____ is the smoke from other people's cigarettes and cigars. **Lesson 25**

2. A _____ is a drug used to treat an illness or injury. **Lesson 23**

3. A _____ _____ is an adult who drinks too much and has wrong actions. **Lesson 24**

4. _____ is letting a drug control you. **Lesson 25**

5. _____ _____ _____ are ways to say NO to wrong decisions. **Lesson 26**

Health Skills

Express Yourself

Draw a poster that shows one way alcohol harms the body.

Learn on Your Own

Call the American Lung Association. Ask them to send you information about chewing tobacco.

Use Thinking Skills

A person who drinks alcohol while driving is more likely to have an accident. Why is this true?

Be a Good Citizen

Write a pledge that you will be drug-free. Sign the pledge. Ask your friends to sign the pledge.

Communicable and Chronic Diseases

Lesson 27
Keep Germs Away

Lesson 28
Habits and Disease

Lesson 29
It's Hard to Breathe

Learn Health Facts

Practice this standard at the end of this unit.

1. Study and learn health facts.
Tell three ways to prevent cancer.

2. Ask questions if you do not understand health facts.
Ask your teacher a question about cancer.

3. Answer questions to show you understand health facts. Answer this question: Why should you wear sunscreen on a sunny day?

4. Use health facts to practice life skills.
Tell what you will do to practice this life skill:
I will choose habits that prevent cancer.

Keep Germs Away

Life Skills

- I will protect myself and others from germs.
- I will learn symptoms and treatment for diseases.

Germs are tiny living things that can make you sick. Germs cause colds and sore throats. Germs can be spread from you to someone else. Germs can be spread from someone else to you.

What You Will Be Able to Do

- Tell how to protect yourself and others from germs.

- Tell ways to get well if you have a disease caused by germs.

Words You Will Learn

- **Germs** are tiny living things that can make you sick.

- **Lyme disease** is a disease that can harm your brain and heart.

- A **symptom** is a change from normal in a person's health.

How Can I Protect Myself and Others from Germs?

Wash your hands often. Wash your hands after you use the bathroom. Wash your hands before you prepare food and eat.

Cover your mouth and nose when you sneeze or cough. Use a tissue. Wash your hands afterwards.

Keep your fingers out of your eyes, nose, and mouth.

Keep objects such as pencils out of your mouth.

Lyme Disease

Ticks can carry germs. These germs can cause Lyme disease. **Lyme (LYM) disease** is a disease that can harm your brain and heart. Wear a lotion or spray to keep ticks off your body.

Wash your hands often.

Cover your mouth and nose when you sneeze.

How Can I Get Well If I Have a Disease Caused by Germs?

Tell an adult if you have symptoms.

A **symptom** (SIM·tuhm) is a change from normal in a person's health. A sore throat is a symptom. An upset stomach is a symptom. A symptom might mean you have a disease caused by germs.

See a doctor if you need to.

Your parents or guardian might decide to take you to a doctor.

Take any medicine your parent or guardian gives you.

Get plenty of rest.

Drink lots of liquids.

Use... Guidelines for Making Responsible Decisions™

Situation:

Your friend has a cold. She puts her pencil in her mouth. You forgot your pencil. Your friend says you can use her pencil.

Response:

Answer the questions in bold.

1. **Is it healthful to use your friend's pencil?**

2. Is it safe to use your friend's pencil?

3. Do you follow rules and laws if you use your friend's pencil?

4. **Do you show respect for yourself if you use your friend's pencil?**

5. Do you follow your family's guidelines if you use your friend's pencil?

6. **Do you show good character if you use your friend's pencil?**

What is the responsible decision?

Lesson 27

Review

Health Questions

1. What are four ways you can protect yourself and others from germs? **page 157**

2. What are five ways to get well if you have a disease caused by germs? **page 158**

Habits and Disease

Life Skills

- **I will choose habits that prevent heart disease.**
- **I will choose habits that prevent cancer.**

A habit is the way you do something most of the time. A disease is an illness. You can prevent disease when you choose certain habits.

What You Will Be Able to Do

- Explain how you can prevent heart disease.
- Explain how you can prevent cancer.

Words You Will Learn

- **Heart disease** is a disease of the heart and blood vessels.

- **Cancer** is a disease in which harmful cells grow.

- A **sunscreen** is a spray or lotion that protects you from the sun's harmful rays.

How Can I Prevent Heart Disease?

Heart disease is a disease of the heart and blood vessels. Choose habits now to prevent heart disease when you are older.

Get plenty of exercise. Exercise makes your heart strong.

Do not smoke or breathe secondhand smoke. The nicotine in tobacco makes your heart work harder.

Eat low-fat foods. Eating too much fat can cause heart disease. The fat sticks on the walls of blood vessels. The blood vessels cannot carry as much blood. Your heart does not get enough oxygen.

Artery without fat sticking on its walls.

Artery with fat sticking on its walls.

How Can I Prevent Cancer?

Cancer (KAN·ser) is a disease in which harmful cells grow. Choose habits now to prevent cancer when you are older.

Wear sunscreen to protect yourself from the sun. A **sunscreen** is a spray or lotion that protects you from the sun's harmful rays. Wear a sunscreen that has a sun protection factor (SPF) of 15 or higher.

Do not smoke or breathe secondhand smoke. Tobacco smoke can change healthy cells. It can cause cancer.

Eat fruits, vegetables, and grains. They help you have a daily bowel movement.

I Love My Heart

What You Will Need: Construction paper, crayons, and scissors

1. **Cut out a heart from construction paper.**

2. **Draw a sport shoe in the center.**

3. **Show your heart to the class.**

4. **Tell the class your favorite exercise.**

Lesson 28

Review

Health Questions

1. What are three habits that prevent heart disease? **page 161**

2. What are three habits that prevent cancer? **page 162**

It's Hard to Breathe

Life Skills

- I will tell ways to care for asthma.
- I will tell ways to care for allergies.

Some children have asthma or an allergy. **Asthma** (AZ·muh) is a condition in which the air passages become narrow. An **allergy** (AL·uhr·jee) is the body's overreaction to something you breathe, touch, or eat.

What You Will Be Able to Do

- List things that can make asthma and allergies worse.
- Tell ways you can care for asthma and allergies.

Words You Will Learn

- **Asthma** is a condition in which the air passages become narrow.
- An **allergy** is the body's overreaction to something you breathe, touch, or eat.

What Things Can Make Asthma and Allergies Worse?

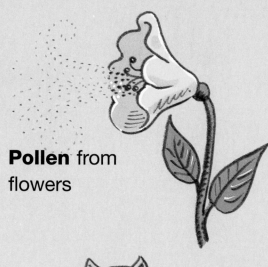

Pollen from flowers

Dust mites that live in carpets and mattresses

Dead skin flakes from **animals with fur**

Household products used to clean your home

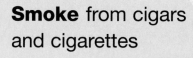

Smoke from cigars and cigarettes

Small bits of ashes from **fireplaces** and **wood-burning stoves**

How Can I Care for Allergies and Asthma?

Suppose you have asthma or an allergy. Suppose someone you know has asthma or an allergy. Here are ways to care for asthma and allergies.

- **Have regular checkups.**
- **Do what your doctor tells you to do.**
- **Take medicine as your doctor tells you.**
- **Stay away from things that cause your body to overreact.**

Health Words

An **allergy** is the body's overreaction to something you breathe, touch, or eat.

Allergy Guessing Game

What You Will Need: Paper and pencil

1. **Number a sheet of paper from 1–6.**

2. **Read each clue below.** Each clue is something that can make asthma and allergies worse.

3. **Write the cause.** Look at page 165 to help you.

---

1. It's the stuff that comes out in the spring from a flower.

2. You use them to clean your sink, bathtub, and shower.

3. It's cozy and warm but can cause you to sneeze.

4. When someone lights up, you say, "Put it out, please."

5. It's gentle, it purrs, it rubs on your feet.

6. You get rid of this often to keep your house neat.

Lesson 29
Review

Health Questions

1. What are three things that can make asthma and allergies worse? **page 165**

2. What are four ways you can care for asthma and allergies? **page 166**

Unit 7

Review

Health Questions

1. What are four ways you can protect yourself and others from germs?
Lesson 27 page 157

2. What are five ways to get well if you have a disease caused by germs?
Lesson 27 page 158

3. What are three habits that prevent heart disease?
Lesson 28 page 161

4. What are three habits that prevent cancer?
Lesson 28 page 162

5. What are three things that can make asthma and allergies worse?
Lesson 29 page 165

Guidelines for Making Responsible Decisions™

You go to the pool to swim with a friend. You forgot your sunscreen. What should you do? **Answer the questions in bold.**

1. **Is it healthful not to wear sunscreen?**

2. Is it safe not to wear sunscreen?

3. Do you follow rules and laws if you do not wear sunscreen?

4. **Do you show respect for yourself if you do not wear sunscreen?**

5. **Do you follow your family's guidelines if you do not wear sunscreen?**

6. **Do you show good character if you do not wear sunscreen?**

What is the responsible decision?

Health Words

Number a sheet of paper from 1–5. Write the word that belongs in the blank. Use the health words in the box.

> **asthma**
>
> **cancer**
>
> **heart disease**
>
> **sunscreen**
>
> **symptom**

1. A _____ is a change from normal in a person's health. **Lesson 27**

2. A _____ is a spray or lotion that protects you from the sun's harmful rays. **Lesson 28**

3. _____ is a condition in which the air passages become narrow. **Lesson 29**

4. _____ _____ is a disease of the heart and blood vessels. **Lesson 28**

5. _____ is a disease in which harmful cells grow. **Lesson 28**

Health Skills

Express Yourself

Draw a picture of a big sun. Write one way to protect yourself from the sun. Write it inside the sun.

Learn on Your Own

Go to a grocery store with your parents or guardian. Find five foods with the label "low-fat."

Use Thinking Skills

Allergies can be caused by animals with fur and by birds. What are three pets that would not cause an allergy?

Be a Good Citizen

Suppose there is no soap in the restroom. Tell your teacher when this happens.

Consumer and Community Health

Lesson 30
Don't Fall for Wrong Information

Lesson 31
That's Entertainment

Lesson 32
Know Health Helpers

Get What You Need for Good Health

Practice this standard at the end of this unit.

1. **Name what you need for good health.**
   Draw a picture of a toothbrush.

2. **Find what you need for good health.**
   Tell two places where you might get a toothbrush.

3. **Check out what you need for good health.**
   Ask a parent or guardian to check out toothbrushes with you. Which one is right for you?

4. **Take action when something is not right.**
   Suppose you got a new toothbrush. The package has been opened. What action might you take?

Don't Fall for Wrong Information

Life Skills

- I will check out ways to learn health facts.
- I will check out ads.
- I will choose safe and healthful products.

Some information you see or hear about health is wrong. You need health facts. A **health fact** is a true statement about health. Use health facts to decide what to buy.

What You Will Be Able to Do

- Tell places you can get health facts.
- List questions to ask when you check out an ad.
- Choose safe and healthful products.

Words You Will Learn

- A **health fact** is a true statement about health.

- A **Web site** is a computer system that has information.

- A **health helper** is a person who helps you stay healthy.

- An **ad** is pictures or words that try to get you to buy something.

Where Can I Find Health Facts?

Read books and magazines.

Some magazines have health facts.
Encyclopedias have health facts.
Library books have health facts.
Ask an adult to help you choose.

Locate a Web site on the computer.

A **Web site** is a computer system that has information. Get permission from your parents or guardian. Find health facts on a Web site. Ask an adult to help you.

Ask a health helper.

A **health helper** is a person who helps you stay healthy. Talk to your doctor or school nurse. They can answer your questions.

What Questions Should I Ask When I See or Hear an Ad?

An **ad** is pictures or words that try to get you to buy something. Ask three questions when you see or hear an ad.

What health facts are in the ad?

You see an ad on TV for a new cereal. The ad says the cereal is low in fat. This is a health fact.

What health facts are left out of the ad?

The new cereal has a lot of sugar. But the ad does not tell you about the sugar.

Do I really need the product in the ad?

The cereal is a kind of health product. You do not need to buy a cereal that has lots of sugar.

Check Out TV Ads

What You Will Need: Paper and pencil

1. **Choose a TV ad that tries to sell you cereal.**

2. **Write the answers to the questions in the box.** Ask your parents or guardian to help you.

3. **Share your answers with your class.**

---

1. What is a health fact in the ad?

2. What is a health fact that is left out? Go to a store. Read the food label to find a health fact that is left out.

3. Do you need the cereal?

Lesson 30 Review

Health Questions

1. What are three places where you can find health facts? **page 173**

2. What are three questions you should ask when you see or hear an ad? **page 174**

That's Entertainment

Life Skills

- **I will choose healthful entertainment.**
- **I will make wise choices about time and money.**

Entertainment is something you see or do that interests you. TV shows, computer games, and board games are entertainment. **Healthful entertainment** is entertainment that keeps your mind and body healthy.

What You Will Be Able to Do

- List guidelines for choosing computer games.

- Make a health plan to choose TV shows that follow guidelines for healthful entertainment.

Words You Will Learn

- **Entertainment** is something you see or do that interests you.

- **Healthful entertainment** is entertainment that keeps your mind and body healthy.

- A **CD-ROM** is a computer disc that stores computer programs.

What Are Guidelines for Choosing Computer Games?

Have you ever played a computer game? Computer games might come on a CD-ROM. A **CD-ROM** (SEE·DEE·RAHM) is a computer disc that stores computer programs.

Some computer games are better to play than others. These computer games keep your mind alert. They help you learn facts. These computer games encourage you to act in responsible ways.

Guidelines for Choosing Computer Games

1. The computer game has the OK of your parents or guardian.

2. The computer game shows characters who follow family guidelines.

3. The computer game shows characters who act in responsible ways.

4. The computer game leaves out violence.

5. The computer game leaves out bad words.

My Health Plan

**Use the same life skill.
Make your own Health Plan.**

Choose TV Shows That Follow Guidelines for Healthful Entertainment

Life Skill

I will make wise choices about time and money.

Name _____

Date _____

My Plan: I will talk to my parents or guardian. They will tell me how much TV I can watch each day. They will help me choose TV programs wisely. I will use the Guidelines for Choosing Healthful Entertainment.

Guidelines for Choosing Healthful Entertainment

1. The TV program has the OK of your parents or guardian.

2. The TV program shows characters who follow family guidelines.

3. The TV program shows characters who act in responsible ways.

4. The TV program leaves out violence.

5. The TV program leaves out bad words.

What I Did:

I will write how much TV I can watch each day.
*I can watch one hour of TV each day.*_____

I will write three TV shows that follow the guidelines.

1. _____

2. _____

3. _____

Turn Off the TV

What You Will Need: A box with a hole cut out to look like a TV

1. **Write one thing to do besides watch TV.**

2. **Face the class.** Hold the box over your head. Look out through the hole.

3. **Say the following:**

"I've had enough. I'm tired of TV. I'm going to do an activity. I'll _____."

Lesson 31 Review

Health Questions

1. What are five guidelines for choosing computer games? **page 177**

2. What are five guidelines for choosing healthful entertainment? **page 178**

Know Health Helpers

Life Skills

- I will cooperate with health helpers.
- I will check out jobs in health.

A **health helper** is a person who helps you stay healthy. Know who health helpers are. Then you know whom to ask questions about health.

What You Will Be Able to Do

- Tell what health helpers do.
- Tell steps to become a health helper.
- Tell what a volunteer does.

Words You Will Learn

- A **health helper** is a person who helps you stay healthy.

- To **cooperate** is to work together.

- A **volunteer** is a person who helps someone without getting paid.

What Do Health Helpers Do?

To **cooperate** (koh·AH·puh·rayt) is to work together. Cooperate with these health helpers.

School Nurse

The school nurse gives you first aid when you are hurt. The school nurse takes your temperature when you are ill.

Dentist

A dentist checks your teeth for cavities. Your dentist tells you how to take care of your teeth.

Police Officer

A police officer helps you if you are lost. A police officer protects you from people who might harm you.

Steps to Become a Health Helper

Activity

1. **Read the steps to become a health helper.**

2. **Line up with your classmates.**

3. **Take one step every time your teacher names a step.**

STEPS

1. I will talk with my parents or guardian about a job as a health helper.

2. I will talk with a health helper about a job in health.

3. I will read about what the health helper does.

4. I will earn good grades in science.

5. I will earn good grades in health.

6. I will learn how to get along with people.

7. I will take the classes I need to be a health helper.

8. I am a health helper!

What Does a Volunteer Do?

A **volunteer** (vah·luhn·TIR) is a person who helps someone without getting paid. Your parents or guardian might volunteer. They might volunteer to collect money for the American Cancer Society. They might volunteer to serve food in a homeless shelter. Ask your parents or guardian for ways you can volunteer.

Lesson 32
Review

Health Questions

1. What does a school nurse do? What does a dentist do? What does a police officer do? **page 181**

2. What are eight steps you can take to become a health helper? **page 182**

3. What does a volunteer do? **page 183**

Review

Health Questions

1. What are three places where you can find health facts? **Lesson 30 page 173**

2. What are three questions you should ask when you see or hear an ad? **Lesson 30 page 174**

3. What are five guidelines for choosing computer games? **Lesson 31 page 177**

4. What are eight steps you can take to become a health helper? **Lesson 32 page 182**

5. What does a volunteer do? **Lesson 32 page 183**

Guidelines for Making Responsible Decisions™

Your friend wants to watch a TV show that has violence. **Answer the questions in bold.**

1. **Is it healthful to watch violence on TV?**

2. Is it safe to watch violence on TV?

3. Do you follow rules and laws if you watch violence on TV?

4. **Do you show respect for yourself if you watch violence on TV?**

5. **Do you follow your family's guidelines if you watch violence on TV?**

6. **Do you show good character if you watch violence on TV?**

What is the responsible decision?

Health Words

Number a sheet of paper from 1–5. Write the word that belongs in the blank. Use the health words in the box.

> **ad**
>
> **cooperate**
>
> **entertainment**
>
> **health fact**
>
> **health helper**

1. _____ is something you see or do that interests you. **Lesson 31**

2. A _____ _____ is a true statement about health. **Lesson 30**

3. To _____ is to work together. **Lesson 32**

4. A _____ _____ is a person who helps you stay healthy. **Lesson 32**

5. An _____ is pictures or words that try to get you to buy something. **Lesson 30**

Health Skills

Express Yourself

Write the questions you should ask about ads on a sheet of paper. Place the paper near your TV.

Learn on Your Own

Ask your school nurse, "What are three ways I can care for my health?"

Use Thinking Skills

What are some kinds of healthful entertainment you can enjoy with your family?

Be a Good Citizen

Get permission from your parent or guardian. Locate a Web site about health. Write three things you learned. Share them with your family and classmates.

Environmental Health

Lesson 33
Protect the Environment

Lesson 34
Don't Pollute

Lesson 35
Turn Down the Noise

Use Say NO Skills

Practice this standard at the end of this unit.

Pair up with a classmate. Suppose the classmate wants you to paint initials on the school building.

1. **Look directly at the person.**
   Look at your classmate.

2. **Say NO.** Say, "NO, I will not paint my initials on the school building."

3. **Tell why you are saying NO.** Tell why you will not paint your initials.

4. **Repeat your NO if you need to.**
   Say NO again. Repeat your reasons.

5. **Do not change your mind.** Do not give in if your classmate keeps asking you.

Protect the Environment

Life Skills

- **I will help protect my environment.**
- **I will help keep my environment friendly.**

To protect means to keep from harm. Your **environment** (in·VY·ruhn·muhnt) is everything that is around you. You can protect your environment. You can enjoy the environment with others.

What You Will Be Able to Do

- Explain how to protect your environment.

- Explain how to keep your environment friendly.

Words You Will Learn

- Your **environment** is everything that is around you.

- **Resources** are things found in nature that people need.

- A **friendly environment** is an environment in which people share space and get along.

How Can I Protect My Environment?

Keep your environment healthful and safe. Clean up after yourself. Throw trash in trash cans. Do not pour household products down the drain.

Keep your environment beautiful. Do not pick wildflowers. Do not carve your initials on a tree. Do not throw trash on the ground or in the water.

Do not use more than your share of resources. **Resources** are things found in nature that people need. Do not waste water or energy. Then there will be enough for everyone.

How Can I Keep My Environment Friendly?

A **friendly environment** is an environment in which people share space and get along. Here are ways you can keep your environment friendly.

Follow rules and laws. Citizens get along well with others when they follow rules and laws. A citizen is a person who lives in a certain town.

Show you care about other people's belongings. Do not borrow things unless you ask first. Do not play in your neighbor's yard without asking. Keep your dog on a leash.

Do not use put-downs. Do not call others mean names. Do not make fun of people who are different from you.

Friendly Sash

What You Will Need: Crayons, scissors, stapler, and poster paper cut into sashes

1. **Write one way to keep your environment friendly on a sash.**

2. **Place the sash over one shoulder and under the other arm.** The sash will go across your chest. Staple the ends together.

3. **Wear your sash for one day.**

Activity

Lesson 33 Review

Health Questions

1. What are three ways you can protect your environment? **page 189**

2. What are three ways you can keep your environment friendly? **page 190**

Don't Pollute

Life Skills

- **I will help stop pollution.**
- **I will not waste energy and resources.**

Litter is trash that is thrown on land or in water. Litter is a form of pollution. **Pollution** (puh·LOO·shuhn) is anything that can harm the air, water, or land. You can help stop pollution.

What You Will Be Able to Do

- Tell ways to stop pollution.
- Tell ways to save energy and resources.

Words You Will Learn

- **Litter** is trash that is thrown on land or in water.

- **Pollution** is anything that can harm the air, water, or land.

- To **recycle** is to use something again.

How Can I Help Stop Pollution?

Keep the air in your home safe.
Talk to your parents or guardian about having a "no smoking" rule. Smoke causes air pollution.

Keep the land clean. Do not throw trash on the ground. Litter causes land pollution.

Keep the water safe. Do not pour unsafe household products down the drain. Unsafe products cause water pollution. Your parents or guardian can tell you what products are unsafe.

How Can I Save Energy and Resources?

Energy is heat and power. Energy is used to heat homes. It is used to run appliances. Resources are things found in nature that people need. Water is a resource. You need water to drink. Trees are a resource. They are used to make paper and wood. Here are ways you can save energy and resources.

Use less energy. Turn off lights and machines when you are not using them.

Use less water. Turn off the water when you brush your teeth.

Use less paper. Write on both sides of a sheet of paper.

Count on Recycling

1. **Read the box below.** The box lists products that you can recycle. To **recycle** (ree·SY·kuhl) is to use something again.

2. **Ask your parents or guardian to help you.** Find three products in your home that you can recycle.

Products That You Can Recycle
- Aluminum cans
- Plastic grocery bags
- Recyclable plastic containers

A recyclable plastic container has "1" or "2" marked on the bottom.

Lesson 34 Review

Health Questions

1. What are three ways you can help stop pollution? **page 193**

2. What are three ways you can save energy and resources? **page 194**

Turn Down the Noise

Life Skill

• **I will keep noise down.**

Noise is sound that bothers you. Noise can be a loud sound. The sound of a jet engine might bother you. Noise can be a soft sound. Someone talking while you read might bother you.

What You Will Be Able to Do

• Discuss reasons you need to keep noise down.

• Make a health plan to keep noise down.

• Tell when you need to wear ear protectors.

Words You Will Learn

• **Noise** is sound that bothers you.

• **Hearing loss** is not being able to hear sounds you should hear.

• **Ear protectors** are coverings worn over the ears to block sounds.

Why Do I Need to Keep Noise Down?

Noise can cause stress. Stress is the way your body reacts when you have strong feelings. Suppose you hear loud noises. Your heart beats faster. Your blood pressure goes up. Stress from noise can make you tired.

Noise can cause hearing loss. **Hearing loss** is not being able to hear sounds you should hear. Suppose you often listen to loud music. The loud music harms your hearing. You cannot hear some everyday sounds.

Noise can cause you to make mistakes. Suppose you are studying. You hear a radio in the next room. You cannot think clearly. You make mistakes on your homework.

My Health Plan

Use the same life skill. Make your own Health Plan.

Keep Noise Down

Life Skill

I will keep noise down.

Name _____

Date _____

My Plan: There are four actions I can take to keep noise down. I will follow these actions for a week.

Actions to Keep Noise Down

1. I will not play music loud.
2. I will keep the sound low on my headphones.
3. I will keep the sound low on the TV.
4. I will not yell indoors except to warn someone of danger.

What I Did: I will use this calendar. I will put a check on the days I followed these actions.

My Calendar

M	T	W	Th	F	S	S
✓	✓	✓	✓	✓	✓	✓

When Do I Need to Wear Ear Protectors?

Ear protectors are coverings worn over the ears to block sounds. You do not need to wear ear protectors when you hear safe sounds. Wear ear protectors when you hear sounds that can cause hearing loss.

Some Safe Sounds

- A whisper
- A quiet room
- Rainfall
- A conversation
- A dishwasher

Some Sounds That Can Cause Hearing Loss

- A jackhammer
- A jet plane takeoff
- Loud music
- A chain saw
- A lawnmower

Lesson 35 Review

Health Questions

1. What are three reasons to keep noise down? **page 197**

2. What are four ways you can keep noise down? **page 198**

3. When do you need to wear ear protectors? **page 199**

Review

Health Questions

1. What are three ways you can protect your environment? **Lesson 33 page 189**

2. What are three ways you can keep your environment friendly? **Lesson 33 page 190**

3. What are three ways you can help stop pollution? **Lesson 34 page 193**

4. What are three reasons to keep noise down? **Lesson 35 page 197**

5. What are four ways you can keep noise down? **Lesson 35 page 198**

Guidelines for Making Responsible Decisions™

You are washing the family car. You turn off the water when you soap up the car. Your brother says, "Let the water run."
Answer the questions in bold.

1. Is it healthful to let the water run?

2. Is it safe to let the water run?

3. Do you follow rules and laws if you let the water run?

4. Do you show respect for yourself if you let the water run?

5. **Do you follow family guidelines if you let the water run?**

6. **Do you show good character if you let the water run?**

What is the responsible decision?

Health Words

Number a sheet of paper from 1–5. Write the word that belongs in the blank. Use the health words in the box.

environment

litter

noise

pollution

recycle

1. _____ is anything that can harm the air, water, or land. **Lesson 34**

2. Your _____ is everything that is around you. **Lesson 33**

3. To _____ is to use something again. **Lesson 34**

4. _____ is sound that bothers you. **Lesson 35**

5. _____ is trash that is thrown on land or in water. **Lesson 34**

Health Skills

Express Yourself

Write down three things you like about the outdoors.

Learn on Your Own

Get permission from your parents or guardian to use a computer. Locate the Internet Web site www.epa.gov. Find the page for kids.

Use Thinking Skills

Suppose you study in a noisy room. What might happen to your grades?

Be a Good Citizen

List ways to keep your environment friendly. Post the list in your classroom.

Injury Prevention and Safety

Lesson 36
Safety First

Lesson 37
Bully Beware

Lesson 38
Safe from Guns and Gangs

Lesson 39
A Guide to First Aid

PRACTICE
HEALTH STANDARD 7

Help Others to Be Safe and Healthy

Practice this standard at the end of this unit.

1. **Choose a safe, healthful action.** You might choose: Wear a safety belt when riding in a car.

2. **Tell others about the safe, healthful action.** Tell your family why every one should wear a safety belt when riding in a car.

3. **Do the safe, healthful action.** Wear a safety belt every time you ride in a car. Show others you choose this safe action.

4. **Help others to do the safe, healthful action.** Look the next time your family rides in a car. Check to see that everyone wears a safety belt.

Safety First

- I will follow safety rules for home and school.
- I will follow safety rules for when I play.
- I will follow safety rules for when I ride in a car.
- I will follow safety rules for bad weather.

A rule is a guide to help you do the right thing. A **safety rule** is a rule to help you stay safe. Safety rules keep you and others from getting hurt.

Words You Will Learn

- A **safety rule** is a rule to help you stay safe.

- A **poison** is a substance that harms the mind and body.

- A **safety belt** is a lap belt and a shoulder belt.

What You Will Be Able to Do

- Tell safety rules to protect you.

How Can I Stay Safe at Home?

Follow Safety Rules to Prevent Poisoning

A **poison** (POY·zuhn) is a substance that harms the mind and body. Bug sprays, gasoline, and bleach are poisons.

1. Do not touch poisons.

2. Do not breathe in poisons.

3. Ask your parent or guardian to help you know whether something is a poison.

Follow Safety Rules to Prevent Falls

1. Put your toys and books away.

2. Do not run in your home.

Follow Safety Rules for Bad Weather

1. Stay indoors if you hear thunder or see lightning.

2. Do not use the telephone during a thunderstorm.

3. Keep away from the water in sinks and bathtubs.

Do not touch poisons.

Fire Safety Rules

Activity

1. **Read the poem about fire safety rules.**

2. **Find the hidden fire safety rules in the poem.**

3. **Make a list of the fire safety rules with your classmates.** Your teacher will write the list on the chalkboard.

FIRE SAFETY RULES

If a fire breaks out,
get out fast as you can.
Remember to follow
your fire escape plan.

Don't stop to look around
for a favorite toy.
Fires spread fast
and fast they destroy.

Try if you can
to go out a door.
Smoke always rises
so crawl on the floor.

Go to the meeting place
that is outside.
And do not think about
going back inside.

Fire Escape Plan

Make a plan with your family **BEFORE** a fire starts. Know two ways to escape from each room. Choose a place to meet outside.

If Your Clothes Catch Fire

Stop! Do not run.

Drop! Drop to the floor or ground.

Roll! Roll to put out the fire.

How Can I Stay Safe When I Travel?

Follow Safety Rules When You Walk Somewhere

1. Walk with another person.

2. Walk on sidewalks. Do not walk in the street.

3. Cross streets at crosswalks or at corners. Look both ways before you cross streets.

Follow Safety Rules When You Ride in a Car

1. Wear a safety belt. A **safety belt** is a lap belt and a shoulder belt.

2. Ride in the back seat.

3. Lock your door when you are inside.

How Can I Stay Safe When I Play?

Follow Safety Rules When You Ride Your Bike

1. Tell your parents or guardian where you will ride your bike.

2. Wear a bicycle helmet.

3. Do not ride in a street or road. Ride on bike paths.

4. Keep both hands on the handlebars.

5. Do not ride double.

6. Use hand signals.

7. Obey stop signs and lights.

8. Stop and look both ways if you cross a street.

9. Ride your bike only in daylight.

10. Ride single file.

Follow Safety Rules When You Swim

1. Swim only when an adult is watching.

2. Do not push, dunk, or shove others. Tell an adult if someone does this to you.

Stick with Playground Safety

What You Will Need: A sticker

1. **Your teacher will make a poster that shows Safety Rules for the Playground.**

2. **Tell a safety rule for the playground.** Put a sticker on the poster next to this safety rule.

Safety Rules for the Playground

1. Go down a slide one at a time.

2. Do not push or shove others.

3. Do not tie ropes or scarves to playground toys.

4. Tell an adult if toys are broken or loose.

Lesson 36 Review

Health Questions

1. What are three safety rules to prevent poisoning? **page 205**

2. What are three safety rules for bad weather? **page 205**

3. What are three safety rules for when you ride in a car? **page 207**

4. What are ten safety rules for when you ride your bike? **page 208**

5. What are four safety rules for the playground? **page 209**

Bully Beware

Life Skills

- **I will protect myself from people who might harm me.**
- **I will follow safety rules to protect myself from violence.**

To beware is to be careful. You need to be careful around some people. Some people might harm you. **Violence** is harm done to people or their belongings.

What You Will Be Able to Do

- Tell ways you can stay safe from a bully.
- Tell ways you can stay safe from strangers.
- Tell what to do if you get an unsafe touch.

Words You Will Learn

- **Violence** is harm done to people or their belongings.
- A **bully** is a person who hurts or threatens someone.
- A **stranger** is a person you do not know well.
- An **unsafe touch** is a touch that is not right.

How Can I Stay Safe from a Bully?

A **bully** is a person who hurts or threatens someone. A bully might take your lunch. A bully might say mean things to you. A bully might try to start a fight.

Follow Rules to Stay Safe from a Bully

1. Tell your parent, guardian, or another trusted adult about a bully.

2. Do not try to get even with a bully.

3. Stay away from a bully.

How Can I Stay Safe from a Stranger?

A **stranger** is a person you do not know well. Most strangers are kind. But some strangers might harm you.

Suppose you are home with only an older brother or sister. A stranger might come to your door. A stranger might call.

Follow Rules to Stay Safe from Strangers Who Come to Your Home

1. Do not let anyone into your home. Keep the door locked.

2. Phone your parents or guardian if a stranger comes to the door.

3. Do not tell a caller that your parents or guardian are not home.

4. Do not say your name, address, or telephone number over the phone.

Follow Rules to Stay Safe from Strangers When You Play

1. Tell your parents or guardian where you will play.

2. Do not play alone.

3. Do not talk to a stranger.

4. Run away if a stranger talks to you.

Do not play alone.

What Are Rules If You Get an Unsafe Touch?

An **unsafe touch** is a touch that is not right. Someone might tickle you in a way you do not want to be tickled. Someone might touch a private body part. A private body part is a body part that your bathing suit covers.

Follow Rules If You Get an Unsafe Touch

1. Tell the person to stop.

2. Yell as loud as you can.

3. Run away.

4. Tell your parents, guardian, or another trusted adult right away.

Lesson 37

Health Questions

1. What are three rules to follow to stay safe from a bully? **page 211**

2. What are eight rules to follow to stay safe from a stranger? **page 212**

3. What are four rules to follow if you get an unsafe touch? **page 213**

Safe from Guns and Gangs

- **I will stay safe from guns.**
- **I will stay away from gangs.**

Violence is harm done to people or their belongings. The wrong use of a gun can cause violence. Gangs cause violence.

What You Will Be Able to Do

- Explain rules to stay safe if you find a gun.
- Explain rules to stay away from gangs.

Words You Will Learn

- **Violence** is harm done to people or their belongings.

- A **gang** is a group of people who cause violence.

- A **law** is a rule that protects people in a community.

How Can I Stay Safe If I Find a Gun?

A gunshot wound can kill a person. A gunshot wound can hurt a person for life.

Follow Rules to Stay Safe If You Find a Gun

1. Stop.

2. Do not touch the gun.

3. Get away from the gun.

4. Tell a trusted adult about the gun.

Do Not Act Out Violence When You Play

- Do not point a toy gun at someone.

- Do not pretend your toy gun is a real gun.

- Do not pretend that a pencil in your pocket is a gun.

How Can I Stay Away from Gangs?

A **gang** is a group of people who cause violence. Gang members break laws. A **law** is a rule that protects people in a community. Gang members carry guns and knives. They use and sell drugs. They steal from people.

Follow Rules to Stay Away from Gangs

1. Stay away from a person who belongs to a gang.

2. Say NO if you are asked to join a gang.

3. Do not copy gang members. Do not dress like them. Do not wear the same colors. Do not write the same words.

4. Tell your parents or guardian if a gang member talks to you.

Use... Guidelines for Making Responsible Decisions™

Situation:

Your friend wants you to dress like a gang member. He wants you to wear the same colors as gang members.

Response:

Answer the questions in bold.

1. Is it healthful to dress like a gang member?

2. **Is it safe to dress like a gang member?**

3. Do you follow rules and laws if you dress like a gang member?

4. **Do you show respect for yourself if you dress like a gang member?**

5. **Do you follow your family's guidelines if you dress like a gang member?**

6. **Do you show good character if you dress like a gang member?**

What is the responsible decision?

Lesson 38

Health Questions

1. What are four ways to stay safe if you find a gun? **page 215**

2. What are four ways to stay away from gangs? **page 216**

A Guide to First Aid

Life Skill

• **I will learn first aid.**

First aid is help for someone who is suddenly hurt or sick. You can know what to do if you or someone else needs first aid.

What You Will Be Able to Do

• Make a health plan to call for help if someone gets hurt.

• Tell what to do for a cut, nosebleed, animal bite, and bee sting.

Words You Will Learn

• **First aid** is help for someone who is suddenly hurt or sick.

• **9-1-1** is a phone number to call for help.

My Health Plan

**Use the same life skill.
Make your own Health Plan.**

Call for Help

 **Life Skill** **I will learn first aid.**

Name _____

Date _____

My Plan: I will practice how to make a phone call to get help. I will ask my parents or guardian to practice with me. I will not use a real phone.

How to Make a Call for Help

1. Find an adult.

2. Go to a phone if you cannot find an adult. Dial 9-1-1 or 0 (operator).

3. Say your name and address to the person who answers.

4. Tell what happened.

5. Listen to what the person tells you to do.

6. Do not hang up until you are told to do so.

9-1-1 is a phone number to call for help. Some towns do not have 9-1-1 service. You can call 0 (operator) if you do not have 9-1-1 service.

What I Did: I will memorize how to call for help. I will practice calling for help three times. I will write 9-1-1 on the lines each time I practice.

1. 9-1-1 _____

2. _____

3. _____

What Should I Do If I Get a Cut?

Use First Aid If You Get a Cut

Tell an adult when you get a cut or scrape. Wash the cut with soap and water. Washing will remove some of the germs on the skin around the cut.

Next, press a clean cloth on the cut. This will stop the bleeding. Put a bandage on the cut. The adult will call a doctor if the cut does not stop bleeding.

Use First Aid If You Help Someone Who Gets a Cut

Wear throw-away gloves if you touch someone's blood. Blood can have germs in it. Do not touch your eyes, nose, or mouth. Do not eat or drink.

What Should I Do If I Have a Nosebleed?

Use First Aid If You Have a Nosebleed

Tell an adult if you have a nosebleed. Sit down and lean forward. Pinch your nose shut for ten minutes. Breathe through your mouth. Spit out any blood. The adult will call a doctor if your nose does not stop bleeding.

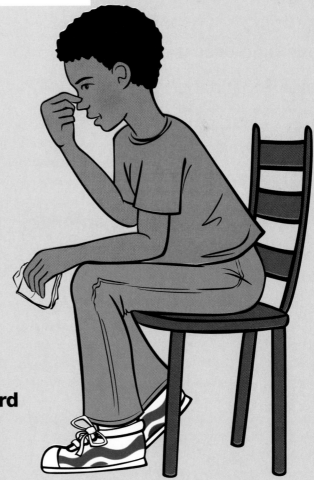

Sit down and lean forward if you have a nosebleed.

What Should I Do If an Animal Bites Me?

Stay away from strange dogs, cats, and other animals. Do not tease animals. Do not bother a pet while it is eating.

Use First Aid If an Animal Bites You

Suppose a dog or another animal bites you. Tell an adult. Wash the bite with soap and water. Place a bandage over the bite. The adult might take you to a doctor.

Most animals are friendly. Treat animals in kind ways.

What Should I Do If I Get a Bee Sting?

Use First Aid If a Bee Stings You

Suppose a bee or wasp stings you. Tell an adult right away. The adult will remove the bee stinger from your skin. Do not try to get it out yourself. The adult will place something cold over the sting.

Remove a bee stinger. Clean the area with soap and water.

Lesson 39 Review

Health Questions

1. What are the six steps to make a call for help? **page 219**

2. What are four things you should do if you get a cut? **page 220**

3. What are five things you should do if you have a nosebleed? **page 221**

4. What are three things you should do if an animal bites you? **page 222**

5. What are four things you should do if you get a bee sting? **page 223**

Health Questions

1. What are ten safety rules for when you ride your bike? **Lesson 36 page 208**

2. What are eight rules to follow to stay safe from a stranger? **Lesson 37 page 212**

3. What are four ways to stay away from gangs? **Lesson 38 page 216**

4. What are the six steps to make a call for help? **Lesson 39 page 219**

5. What are three things you should do if an animal bites you? **Lesson 39 page 222**

Guidelines for Making Responsible Decisions™

A classmate trips you on the school bus. She says she will beat you up if you tell an adult. **Answer the questions in bold.**

1. Is it healthful if you do not tell an adult?

2. **Is it safe if you do not tell an adult?**

3. Do you follow rules and laws if you do not tell an adult?

4. **Do you show respect for yourself if you do not tell an adult?**

5. **Do you follow family guidelines if you do not tell an adult?**

6. **Do you show good character if you do not tell an adult?**

What is the responsible decision?

Health Words

Number a sheet of paper from 1–5. Write the word that belongs in the blank. Use the health words in the box.

first aid
gang
poison
safety rule
stranger

1. A _____ is a substance that harms the mind and body. **Lesson 36**

2. A _____ is a group of people who cause violence. **Lesson 38**

3. A _____ is a person you do not know well. **Lesson 37**

4. _____ _____ is help for someone who is suddenly hurt or sick. **Lesson 39**

5. A _____ _____ is a rule to help you stay safe. **Lesson 36**

Health Skills

Express Yourself

Memorize what you should do if you find a gun. Say it out loud with your friends.

Learn on Your Own

Ask your school nurse how you can make your school safer.

Use Thinking Skills

Why should you never ride your bike at night?

Be a Good Citizen

Make a fire escape plan with your parents or guardian. Tape it to the refrigerator.

Glossary

Sound	As in	Symbol	Example
ă	cat, tap	a	allergy (AL·er·jee)
ā	may, same	ay	brain (BRAYN)
a	wear, dare	ehr	character (KEHR·ik·tuhr)
ä	father, top	ah	adopt (uh·DAHPT)
ar	car, park	ar	heart (HART)
ch	chip, touch	ch	checkup (CHE·kuhp)
ĕ	bet, test	e	memory (MEM·ree)
ē	pea, need	ee	disease (di·ZEEZ)
er	perk, hurt	er	exercise (EK·ser·syz)
g	go, big	g	grooming (GROOM·ing)
ĭ	tip, live	i	disability (DI·suh·BI·luh·tee)
ī	side, by	y, eye	carbohydrates (kar·boh·HY·drayts)
j	job, edge	j	germs (JERMZ)
k	cook, ache	k	cavity (KA·vuh·tee)
ō	bone, know	oh	overfat (OH·ver·FAT)
ô	more, pour	or	resource (REE·sors)
ȯ	saw, all	aw	alcoholism (AL·kuh·HAW·LI·zuhm)
oi	coin, toy	oy	poison (POY·zuhn)
ou	out, now	ow	power (POW·er)
s	see, less	s	safety (SAYF·tee)
sh	she, mission	sh	pollution (puh·LOO·shuhn)
ŭ	cup, dug	uh	drug (DRUHG)
u	wood, pull	u	bully (BUL·ee)
ü	rule, union	oo	tutor (TOO·ter)
w	we, away	w	water (WAH·ter)
y	you, yard	yu	excuse (ik·SKYOOS)
z	zone, raise	z	nerves (NERVZ)
zh	vision, measure	zh	decision (di·SI·zhuhn)
ə	around, mug	uh	afraid (uh·FRAYD)

9-1-1: a phone number to call for help.

A

ad: pictures or words that try to get you to buy something.

addiction: letting a drug control you.

adopt: to bring a child from other parents into your family.

afraid: feeling scared.

age: to grow older.

alcohol: a drug found in some drinks that slows down the body.

allergy (AL·uhr·jee): the body's overreaction to something you breathe, touch, or eat.

angry: feeling very upset with someone or something.

asthma (AZ·muh): a condition in which the air passages become narrow.

B

bones: strong, hard body parts that support the soft body parts.

brain: the body part that sends and receives messages to and from all parts of your body.

bully: a person who hurts or threatens someone.

C

cancer (KAN·ser): a disease in which harmful cells grow.

cavity: a hole in a tooth.

CD-ROM (SEE·DEE·RAHM): a computer disc that stores computer programs.

character (KEHR·ik·tuhr): telling the truth, showing respect, and being fair.

checkup: a check by your doctor to learn how healthy you are.

chore: a small job.

conflict: a disagreement.

cool-down: easy activity after you exercise.

cooperate (koh·AH·puh·rayt): to work together.

D

diet: the foods you usually eat.

Dietary Guidelines: guidelines for eating to help you stay healthy.

disease (di·ZEEZ): an illness.

divorce (duh·VOHRS): the end of a marriage.

drug: something that changes the way your mind or body works.

drug-free: to say NO to drugs that are against the law, to stay away from people who use drugs in wrong ways, and to stay away from parties where people are using drugs in wrong ways.

E

ear protectors: coverings worn over the ears to block sounds.

entertainment: something you see or do that interests you.

environment: everything that is around you.

even friendship: a friendship in which friends take turns sharing and choosing.

227

excuse: a reason you use to try to get out of being responsible for what you did.

exercise: moving your muscles.

F

family: the group of people to whom you are related.

family guidelines: rules your parents or guardians expect you to follow.

fast food restaurant: a restaurant that serves food quickly.

feelings: the ways you feel inside.

fight: a disagreement in which you pull hair, kick, push, punch or pinch.

first aid: help for someone who is suddenly hurt or sick.

fitness: having your body in top form.

floss: to remove the sticky material from teeth.

food group: foods that are alike.

Food Guide Pyramid: a guide that tells how many servings you need from each food group each day.

food label: a label on a food container that shows facts about the food.

friendly environment: an environment in which people share space and get along.

G

gang: a group of people who cause violence.

germs: tiny living things that can make you sick.

good character (KEHR·ik·tuhr): telling the truth, showing respect, and being fair.

good health: taking care of your body, taking care of your mind, sharing feelings, and getting along with others.

good table manners: polite ways to eat.

grooming: taking care of your body and your appearance.

grow: to become bigger.

H

habit: the way you do something most of the time.

handicapped ramp: a path that makes it easier for people who have special needs to go up and down.

handicapped space: a parking place for the car or van in which a person who has special needs rides.

health: taking care of your body, taking care of your mind, sharing feelings, and getting along with others.

health fact: a true statement about health.

healthful entertainment: entertainment that keeps your mind and body healthy.

healthful weight: the weight that keeps you in good health.

health helper: a person who helps you stay healthy.

health plan: a written plan that helps you practice a life skill.

health record: written information your family keeps about your health.

hearing loss: not being able to hear sounds you should hear.

heart: a body part that pumps blood.

heart disease: a disease of the heart and blood vessels.

heart fitness: having a strong heart muscle so you do not tire easily.

L

law: a rule that protects people in a community.

learn: to get to know about something.

life skill: a healthful action you learn and practice for life.

litter: trash that is thrown on land or in water.

lungs: body parts that help move air in and out of your body.

Lyme (LYM) **disease:** a disease that can harm your brain and heart.

M

medicine: a drug used to treat an illness or injury.

memory: being able to remember things.

mistake: something that is done wrong.

mouthguard: something worn in the mouth to protect the teeth and gums.

muscles: body parts that help you move.

N

nerves: body parts that carry messages to and from your brain to the rest of your body.

nicotine (NI·kuh·teen): a harmful drug found in tobacco.

noise: sound that bothers you.

O

overfat: having too much body fat.

P

pet: an animal that is kept in the home.

poison (POY·zuhn): a substance that harms the mind and body.

pollution (puh·LOO·shuhn): anything that can harm the air, water, or land.

problem drinker: an adult who drinks too much and has wrong actions.

R

recycle (ree·SY·kuhl): to use something again.

remarry: to get married again.

resources: things found in nature that people need.

respect: thinking highly of someone.

responsible decision: a choice you will be proud of.

rest: a short break from activity.

S

safety belt: a lap belt and a shoulder belt.

safety rule: a rule to help you stay safe.

say NO skills: ways to say NO to wrong decisions.

secondhand smoke: smoke from other people's cigarettes and cigars.

self-concept: the feeling you have about yourself.

side effect: an unwanted feeling or illness after taking a medicine.

sleep: a time when you are not awake.

smokeless tobacco: tobacco that is chewed.

snack: a food or drink you have between meals.

stomach: a body part that helps change food so your body can use it.

stranger: a person you do not know well.

stress: the way your body reacts to strong feelings.

stress plan: a health plan to show how you will manage stress.

stretch: an exercise that helps you bend and move easily.

sunscreen: a spray or lotion that protects you from the sun's harmful rays.

symptom (SIM·tuhm): a change from normal in a person's health.

T

true friend: a friend who is responsible and who cares about you.

tutor: a person who gives extra help to some children.

U

unsafe touch: a touch that is not right.

V

violence: harm done to people or their belongings.

vision: how well you see.

volunteer (vah·luhn·TIR): a person who helps someone without getting paid.

W

warm-up: easy activity before you exercise.

Web site: a computer system that has information.

wrong decision: a choice you will not be proud of.

A

Ad, 172, 174
Addiction, 144, 145
Adopt, 52, 54
Afraid, 20, 23
Age, 74
Alcohol, 140–143
Allergy, 164–167
Angry, 20, 22
Animal bites, 222
Animals with fur, 165
Asthma, 164–167

B

Baby, 54–55
Bee sting, 223
Bike riding, 207
Bleeding, 220
Blood vessels, 60, 62
Bones, 68, 69
Brain, 60, 66, 79
Breathing, 164–166
Bully, 210, 211

C

Cancer, 140, 141, 160, 162
Cars, and safety, 208
Cavity, 112, 113
CD-ROM, 177
Character, 10, 12, 16–17
Checkup, 108
Chore, 48, 50
Computer, 177
Conflict, 36, 38
Cool-down, 128, 129
Cooperate, 128, 130, 180, 181
Cut, 220

D

Decisions, 10–15
Diet, 86
Dietary Guidelines, 86, 90–91, 92
Disease, 136, 137, 160–163
Divorce, 52, 53
Drinking, 140–143
Drug, 136
Drug-free, 148, 149
Drugs, 148–151
Dust mites, 165

E

Ear protectors, 196, 199
Ears, 110
Entertainment, 176
Environment, 188–191
Even friendship, 42, 43
Excuse, 16, 18
Exercise, 120–127
Eyes, 109

F

Family, 48, 49
Family guidelines, 48, 49
Fast food restaurant, 92, 94
Fat, 96–97
Feelings, 20–25
Fight, 36, 40
Fireplace ashes, 165
First aid, 218–223
Fitness, 120, 121
Floss, 112, 113, 114
Food, and germs, 100–101
Food group, 86
Food Guide Pyramid, 86–89
Food label, 96, 98
Friendly environment, 188, 190
Friendship, 42–47

G

Gang, 214, 216
Germs, 100–101, 156–159
Good character, 10, 12, 16–17
Good health, 4, 5
Good sport, 130
Good table manners, 100, 102
Grooming, 116, 117
Grow, 68
Gun, 215

H

Habit, 68, 72
Handicapped ramp, 74, 76
Handicapped space, 74, 76
Health, 4, 5
Health checkup, 108
Health fact, 172
Health helper, 172, 173, 180–183
Health plan, 4, 8
Health record, 111

Healthful entertainment, 176
Healthful weight, 96
Hearing loss, 108, 110, 196, 197
Hearing record, 108, 111
Heart, 60, 62
Heart disease, 160, 161
Heart fitness, 120, 124
Household products, 165

L
Law, 214, 216
Learn, 78
Life skill, 4, 7
Litter, 192
Lungs, 60, 61
Lyme disease, 156, 157

M
Manners, 100, 102
Medicine, 136–139
Memory, 78, 79
Mistake, 16, 18
Mouthguard, 112, 113
Muscles, 68, 70, 122–123

N
Nerves, 66
Newborn baby, 54–55
Nicotine, 144, 145
9-1-1, 218, 219
Noise, 196–199
Nosebleed, 221

O
Overfat, 96, 97

P
Peace, 36
Pet, 48, 51
Playground safety, 209
Poison, 204, 205
Pollen, 165
Pollution, 192, 193
Problem drinker, 140, 142

R
Recycle, 192, 195
Remarry, 52, 53
Resources, 188, 189, 194

Respect, 10, 12, 16, 36, 37
Responsible decision, 10, 11, 12–13, 42, 43
Rest, 116, 118
Rule, 204

S
Safety, and exercise, 128–131
Safety belt, 112, 113, 204, 207, 208
Safety rules, 204–209
Say NO skills, 10, 14, 148, 150
Secondhand smoke, 144, 146, 160, 161
Self-concept, 20, 24
Side effect, 136, 138
Sleep, 116, 118
Smoke, and breathing, 165
Smokeless tobacco, 144, 145
Smoking, 144–146
Snack, 92, 93
Stomach, 60, 64
Stranger, 210, 212
Stress, 26–29
Stress plan, 26, 28
Stretch, 120, 122
Sunscreen, 160, 162
Swimming, 207
Symptom, 156, 158

T
Teeth, 112–115
Tobacco, 144–145
True friend, 42, 43
Tutor, 78, 81
TV, 178

U
Unsafe touch, 210, 213

V
Violence, 210, 214
Vision, 108, 109
Volunteer, 180, 183

W
Warm-up, 128, 129
Weather, and safety rules, 208
Weight, 96
Wrong decision, 10, 14